News from the Unconscious Realm

News

from the
Unconscious
Realm

Hard-Nosed Journalism
to Plumb the Depths
of the Psyche

Chester Henry

DAGMAR
MIURA
LOS ANGELES

Published by Dagmar Miura
Los Angeles
www.dagmarmiura.com

News from the Unconscious Realm: Hard-Nosed Journalism to
    Plumb the Depths of the Psyche

First published 2023

ISBN: 978-1-956744-81-1

Introduction

nformation from the dream state has long fascinated our species, often in the hope that these unconscious experiences are prophetic and might aid us in navigating waking life, or at least that our dreams are a meaningful way to gain insight into our lives and our challenges. In the modern era the greatest champion of dream insight was arguably the foundational psychologist Carl Jung. His thinking on dreams differed wildly from that of his mentor Sigmund Freud. Freud theorized that our dreams expressed our forbidden desires, and that the meaning of our dreams was therefore coded and obscured. "You've been dreaming about cigars? You fricking little pervert." Jung wrote of his belief that dreams were the psyche's way of communicating with us openly, in transparent terms, not with hidden meanings. He believed that our dreams contained valuable information, that they were important—and that we should pay attention.

Dream analysis long predates the field of psychology, and anyone who remembers their nightly oneiric adventures knows that the experience strays outside the carefully tended bounds of science and religion into a liminal space akin to mysticism. But what to make of these experiences? Returning to consciousness in the morning with memories of another world is like the mystic's dilemma: How do we relate non-ordinary experiences back to baseline reality? The creators of this book have found a way.

Our era is characterized by a breathtaking amount of misinformation and disinformation. With AI becoming indistinguishable from the human hand—software that can make up prose that's lucid but contains nonsensical facts, and software that can create photographs of events that never happened—our waking reality itself has started to bifurcate and feel malleable. The only way to hold on to an objective version of material reality is to choose our sources carefully. For hundreds of years and still today, journalism has been the torch of truth lighting the way through all the spin, the deep-fakes, the paranoid conspiracy theories. Clearly the best medium to transmit factual information is the unflinching hard-nosed journalism that you'll find in these pages.

This project stems from the beloved website *The Dream Report* that ran from the late 1990s through 2011, and the earlier "Dream Report" column that ran in Japan's *Jezebel* magazine from 1991 to 1998, edited by the august scribe Dagmar Miura, whose publishing venture still bears her name and likeness. Some of the content of these reports thus might feel somewhat dated, featuring phone booths, paper airline and rail tickets, even Windows '97. But the psyche doesn't mess around, and the hard facts in these dispatches are vivid and timeless, as meaningful today as they were when the news first broke.

Like the unconscious realm, this book is essentially nonlinear, and the dispatches can be explored in any order. The index at the back of the book can point you to specific topics covered in these articles. So kick off those shoes, unbutton that top button, lean back in that easy chair, crank open that third-eye chakra, and dive into the metaphysical depths of *News from the Unconscious Realm*.

Dreaming the World into Existence

𝕳 ow much do our dreams matter? The *Seth Material* is a collection of books by the psychic medium Jane Roberts, channeled from a discarnate entity named Seth starting in 1963. Broadly about personal development and the nature of reality, the Seth books were a major driver of the New Age philosophical movement that really got rolling in the 1970s. Seth's essential message was that people literally create our own personal and universal environment, and if we become aware of that, we can begin to create better environments, and make progress in our collective conceptual development.

New Age thinking itself is a major advancement in our conceptual development. Religions in the past focused on the whims of nature, like Ba'al making it rain or withholding it, Yahweh the thunder god terrorizing the land, or the female deity within each mountain that precludes women from working on tunneling crews (the goddess would get jealous and cause a cave-in). Other religions dealt with human foibles, like

Poseidon harassing Odysseus for ten whole years when all the guy wanted was to get home. Later the gods resembled kings and strongmen, that one individual who's in charge of every aspect of your life, even applying the same language: "my lord" and "bwana" and "our father" and "the queen of heaven." But the New Age really did bring a new idea: we're responsible for everything that happens, all the parts of our lives, and we're the ones who can change things.

The New Age feels like the most American kind of spiritual thinking, as it meshes neatly with tenets of American culture—the belief that we're free to achieve absolutely anything, that a self-made person can actualize their full potential, that you can pull yourself up by your own bootstraps. Unlike Bronze Age people dealing with the vagaries of the natural world, or medieval peasants dealing with monarchs and despots, American optimism holds that you're in charge of the conditions of your own life.

Anyway, Seth had a lot to say about dreams. In the book *Dreams, Evolution, and Value Fulfillment* (1986), he explains that the dream world is every bit as valid as our waking life. Far from being imaginary, the unconscious realm is full of ideas and actions, and it's literally the source of our conscious world, the pool that material reality emerges from. To quote *The Nature of Personal Reality* (1974):

> The dream world operates as a creative situation in which probable acts are laid out in actual or symbolic form. From these, you then choose the most appropriate for physical expression.

More succinctly, in *The "Unknown" Reality* (1977), Seth says that our unconscious world is "not only as valid as the exterior one, it is the origin for it." Personally I find it a little annoying that I have to be working in my sleep too. While sleep might help restore the physical body, the psyche is being productive, hard at work formulating, trying out, and rehearsing new beliefs and conditions to manifest in waking life.

Seth even talks about what we call lucid dreaming in this reality-generating process. Again from *The Nature of Personal Reality:*

It is quite possible to take your waking "I" into the dream state, where it will provide you with a preliminary stage in which working hypotheses can be creatively formed and tried out.

Lucid dreaming can be more than just an entertaining somnolent adventure. From *The Nature of the Psyche* (1979):

> Often in the dream state you become truly awake, and grab hold of your spirithood and creaturehood with both hands, so to speak, understanding that each has a far greater reality than you have been led to suppose.

Also in *The Nature of Personal Reality*, Seth says that the sharp division that we've set up between waking and sleeping, between consciousness and unconsciousness, has cut us off from participating more actively in that process. If the boundary were more permeable, there would be a natural flow of conscious and unconscious information between waking and sleep, lending us greater creativity and intuition as well as access to deeper wisdom.

There's also no reason that our waking reality can't be as rich and vivid and diverse as the dream world. From *The Nature of the Psyche:*

> You still try to carry your own cultural versions of reality into the dream state, but the natural heritage of both body and mind escapes such repression—and despite yourselves, in your dreams you come in touch with a greater picture of reality that will not be shunted aside. There is nothing inherent in the waking state that causes it to be so limited.

One caveat about the content of these dispatches: this reporting is perhaps insightful only for the dreamer, Chester Henry, despite the hyperbolic subtitle of this book. From *The Nature of the Psyche:*

> There is little use in trying to discover other levels of your own reality if you insist upon applying the laws of physical life to your own larger experience. Then you will always be in a quandary, and no facts will fit.

All this makes me think we need to tune in to our dreams, and listen to them, and let them inform our waking life. Not everyone has the inclination to dive into lucid dreaming, but with a little practice—try to focus on remembering your dreams when you first wake up—you'll remember more of them, maybe get inspired by them, and perhaps help advance the conceptual development of our species by engaging more with the unconscious realm. Sweet dreams!

Dispatches

Confusion over new coin denomination

LOCAL — While making change in a local shop, a man cited confusion created by an unknown coin. "I assume it's a new coin," the man explained, "and the face value is Þ150. It has five or six sides, a bit like the British coin that's worth 20 pence, or maybe it's 50 pence? I was worried that the clerk, or whoever it was, wouldn't

recognize it as Þ150 and would count it as Þ100."

Man promoted to chief of the Osaka district

LOCAL — A local man reports that the Yakuza crime organization made him the chief of the Osaka district tonight. "I was worried about wearing the right clothes, and making a good impression," the man explained.

. . . . . .

Disagreement over Japan ski facility's merits

Woman seen with new girlfriend

MOUNT FUJI, JAPAN — A man reported walking around a village on the slopes of the august mountain this week and unexpectedly encountering an acquaintance from his college days. The woman was now using a wheelchair, and had changed her appearance dramatically, but was allegedly wearing a familiar jacket. "The coat was mine in eighth or ninth grade," the man explains, "and my father wore it in later years for yard work, when I was at college." The garment was described as "bright blue with red and gray shoulder stripes."

The wheelchair-bound woman was accompanied by a girlfriend, but not the woman she was dating in college. The trio agreed to have coffee, and sat at a café at the foot of a ski hill. The man explained that the ski facility was "tiny, with only one steep run," and the snow was described as gray and slushy. Even though he allegedly ridiculed the ski hill, the women spoke of it "as if it were cool."

Baby Strax album drops

CITY — A local resident reported tonight that his neighbor informed him about a new CD by a band called Baby Strax. "He was raving about how good it is," the man alleges. The album cover was described as displaying the band name in all capital letters, as BABY STRAX, and the liner notes, printed in white text on a black background, were allegedly "just a list of adjectives: slimy • wet • juicy • smelly."

. . . .

Shower denied

CITY — Despite his desire to take a shower, a local man reported this morning that it wasn't possible. "My parents had guests," he explained. "They were little people, the size of children, and they beat me to the shower."

. . . . . .

Chance street encounter leads to rebuke

HALIFAX, CANADA — While strolling on a commercial street in the port city, a tourist reportedly ran into a drag queen that he had met the previous evening in a nightclub. "She was wearing the same green and black outfit as the night before," the man stated. Despite promising to return to the club on another evening, in reality he had "no intention of going back there." The man alleged that when he greeted the drag queen with "Hello," she recog- nized him and responded, "Nut."

New roommate breaks tenancy agreement, traffic rules

MONTREAL — Moving into a temporary apartment with a childhood friend in the Canadian city, a local man was dismayed to find that his new roommate had brought two giant hamsters, even though they had reportedly agreed not to have pets. His new roommate insisted on driving to dinner, allegedly making "so many driving errors." The trip to dinner led all around a hilly area with trees, located in a wide-open space in the middle of a valley. "I think it was under construction," the man explained. "It looked like that icky part of April when everything is melting."

· · · · · ·

Chairman Bill

LOS ANGELES — A local man reported finding himself in a boardroom with an older woman. Wearing thick glasses, she was described as "acting all authoritarian." Eventually the man realized she was Chairman Bill.

[*Editor's note:* The Chairman Bill described in this incident bears no relation to conservative pundit William F. Buckley Jr., who has also been described by that moniker.]

Snow letters stabilized with seeds, sand

UP NORTH — A local man reported that a peer from elementary school convinced him to "write stories in the snow." Trenches had been prepared in the snow that were several inches deep, and the man stated that he wrote in the bottom of the trenches using Japanese characters. When some snow drifted into one of the trenches, the man reportedly assumed that the words would be lost, but his companion explained that they wouldn't be, and as he continued to write, his companion began filling in the trenches with nuts and seeds and sand, explaining that the addition of these materials would protect or preserve the words. The man stated that "I ate some of the peanuts," adding that "they had the little papers on them and they were sandy." When roman letters were required in the writing work, the companion provided them separately, in the form of blue plastic letters.

Backwards tractor wreck

Victim injured, lucid

THE COUNTRYSIDE — A man visiting the area reported following his sister down a gravel road at a high rate of speed. The woman was driving a vehicle that looked like "a backwards tractor," and it was described as "swaying dangerously." The woman reportedly swerved to avoid a dog that was chasing the vehicle, and subsequently lost control. The vehicle then crashed, and she was thrown clear. When the man ran to her, he allegedly found that she might have abdominal injuries but that she was lucid.

Producer keeps sweater

LOS ANGELES — In the pursuit of income, a local man contacted a music company with the goal of becoming a songwriter. The music producer was reportedly skeptical, as the photo attached to his resume was allegedly "animated and amateurish." Nonetheless, the producer retained a sweater that the man had designed, described as "a green 1970s style," and stored it in a drawer along with fashion magazines.

. . . . . .

Pacific cruise leads to eerie city, whale encounter

Crew given just 2,600 years to avoid pirates

SOUTH PACIFIC — A man reported being aboard a large navy ship, accompanied by a small escort ship, cruising in the South Pacific sometime after World War II. From the deck the man and others saw several aircraft in the sky. "They looked modern," he explained, "but they were all the wrong shapes. One had German markings, but that was weird, because the war was over." Those on the ship speculated that perhaps the aircraft were circling to observe local military events, possibly a nuclear-powered ship or a nuclear weapons test.

When the man and others from the ship visited the local town, and entered the nightclub, the lounge singer soon voiced the unspoken suspicion allegedly shared by many: "These planes and these people come from another time." The witness understood this to mean that they were from the future. "We walked around the city," he stated, "and it was familiar, but it was alien." Among the almost-familiar features were "a Day-Glo orange Eiffel Tower with an ornate side wing," which was reportedly smaller and more Gothic in style than the original. "We suspected that the visitors—the aliens—copied it," the man explained.

Another feature was a fountain that rested partly under the corner of a granite building. The man's father allegedly found a fish seemingly floating in the air nearby, but on closer examination, it turned out to be in the water in a part of the fountain that had a vertical water surface. In the area was a passage under the street that bore a

sign that said GLASDOOR. "They meant 'glass door,'" the man explained. "It made me very suspicious of who these people were."

The fish fountain was a kind of puzzle, the man alleged, and he and his companions worked to drag various bulky parts of the fountain into alignment, but encountered much difficulty in the attempt. "We realized the point was to change the city to help save it from destruction by pirates," he explained. "I wanted to take a break, so we took a bus to the edge of town, near the harbor." The landscape in the area, he explained, was like a romanticized oil painting.

At the harbor, a huge green whale, described as "stylized—too high and too short," allegedly leapt out of the water in front of the man and his cohorts. "Our character names were written on its side," the man explained. The names were Sorros, Mayflower, Night Feather, and one more. "I think I was supposed to be Sorros," he explained, "but I liked the other names better." The writing on the whale also allegedly said the date was approximately 1663 BCE, and the numbers were changing quickly. "We had until around 1000 CE to alter things enough to avoid the pirates," the man claimed. The whale writing also reportedly chided the group for abandoning the fountain project: as the whale moved away, it read, "Sorros didn't try hard."

Explosion on apartment stairs

Purple security rope booby-trapped

CITY — Descending the stairs in his apartment building with a group of other tenants, a local man reports tonight that they found a purple security rope across the stairs, barring their descent. At the front of the group, the leader then allegedly attempted to move the rope, and the rope exploded, as it had been booby-trapped. The man stated that at that moment, he'd been looking behind him, avoiding the worst impact of the blast.

"I'd had a vision of this beforehand," the man claimed. The other tenants ran back up the stairs, the police were summoned, and a crowd gathered. "Someone had given me an air pistol," the man stated, "so I fired it to get the rubbernecking children to move along." During the entire aftermath of the explosion, the injured leader's head rested on the witness's feet, "until the ambulance crew arrived."

· · · · · ·

Haircuts lead to overseas flight

OTTAWA, CANADA — Upon arriving at his residence, a local man claimed two college-era peers were in the house, each getting a haircut in a different room. "Dave still had clumps of hair on his chest," the man explained, "and Anne was still mid-haircut." The male visitor's hair was described as "long, and straight, like people wore in the mid-1970s."

Unexpectedly the house morphed into an airplane, painted in a vivid powder-blue livery, and commenced an overseas flight, first taxiing on a local parkway.

· · · · · ·

Blown breakers lead to incense discovery

CITY — A local man and his brother were reported to have blown several breakers in a house. "We were throwing water around as we cleaned the place, and all the breakers just blew," he explained. The floor allegedly started to look like it might collapse, and some of the breakers came back on. When the man went to check the breakers for the laundry room, he claimed that the basement had a faint smell of smoke. When he opened the breaker panel, an incense stick had allegedly been placed in the middle and lit.

· · · · · ·

Antiques spotted
Vegetables for sale

AUSTRALIA — While residing temporarily in an Australian village, a man reported that he took a tour of the grain storage facility, where he spotted "some great antiques," including an ironing board. The man spoke to a couple who were selling vegetables and pork minces about his personal work style. The couple reportedly had lots of leafy greens and seasonal vegetables for sale.

French documentary requires explanation

CITY — A local man reported watching a lengthy and intricate French documentary film on television with his brother. The man allegedly spent much of the time explaining parts of the documentary to his sibling "because my French is better." The film reportedly contained a lot of gray and was described as bordering on the surreal.

Poor cell reception linked to scheduling difficulties, catatonia
Man told "don't come here again"

CANADIAN ROCKIES — A man visiting the area reported that his mother wanted him to meet a Japanese folk musician who played an instrument called the mini shoulder harp. Even though they had a meeting time set up, the man claimed he visited "a day earlier, just for two minutes, to drop in."

Spotty cell reception on winding mountain roads made the task of coordinating his work schedule difficult, the man stated. Asked to teach at a school in a distant city, the witness reports that he "blew it off twice, the second time ten minutes after the class had started." Pulling into an empty parking space, the man left a toddler and a dog in the vehicle while he went to call the school, explaining to the pair, "I'll be quick." Locating a phone booth, he called the school, and claims that the administrator politely told him not to visit again.

Returning to the vehicle after a much longer absence than he'd planned, he found the toddler in good health but acting catatonic. "She could move," he explained, "but refused to speak or show any emotion."

Violent mealtime interruption

OUT WEST — Reportedly anxious to start dinner, a local man collaborated on the meal with his sister and a police officer. "I had cut up the onions and peeled the tomatoes," the man explained, "but I hadn't had time to get more onions or buy tomato paste." The police officer allegedly directed the cooking process. Sources indicate that unexpectedly, a small flatbed truck roared through the town, and an elderly woman, walking with a crutch and wearing what witnesses described as a purple jogging suit, had to jump out of the way. At that point the truck recklessly backed around, witnesses said. "It almost hit us, and we had to scramble to escape it," the man explained.

As the dinner preparers watched, the incident quickly escalated: One of the men in the truck climbed out and attacked the elderly woman and her two companions, allegedly striking her "on the right side of the face" with a sledgehammer. "It was dark," the witness explained, "so I couldn't see in detail, but she had to be seriously injured." The other man from the truck was seen carrying a ragged mutilated bison head, allegedly threatening people with its lone remaining horn. Both perpetrators were described as "obese, wearing jeans, and with beards."

Comedy critic's coupons coveted

Underground commuter spaces alleged

NEW YORK CITY — A comedy critic known as Steve visited the city and, in the words of a local resident, "fell into a touchy-feely relationship with me." Steve reportedly had a copious amount of coupon awards, which other people allegedly tried to obtain, while others claimed to have knowledge of large underground commuter spaces located beneath ski slopes.

· · · · · ·

Breakfast encounters with deity and demon

CITY — A local man claims to have had a conversation with God this morning not long after waking. Seated at the kitchen table, the man reportedly asked the Judeo-Christian deity whether the devil "ever came up," pointing out a dark staircase that led downward. "No sooner had I asked than he actually did come up," the witness explained. Dressed in green, with red hair and a beard, "He looked a lot like Vincent van Gogh." The man explained that he instinctively knew not to look in his eyes, but

nonetheless reported feeling fearful, until the devil eventually left.

Chaotic international meeting

Cleaning, cooking take center stage

TOKAI REGION, JAPAN — A staffer at an air conditioner manufacturing plant attended an international meeting today, and alleged that "all the foreign workers showed up late." Assigned to clean the drawers in the kitchen, and subsequently tasked to make test pancakes, the staffer said that a group of women were conducting a feminist protest at the factory. Over the factory's PA system a song was played that was described as "funkadelic," with lyrics that repeated "Come to the temple / come to the temple."

• • • • • •

Bathroom cleaning, renovations interrupted by controlled demolition

Concrete debris widespread

LOCAL — A local man described cleaning out the toilet in his apartment today "with my arm up to my elbow." Unusual items were allegedly clogging the pipes, including "old makeup containers, inch-long water worms, and small green and yellow bugs all around." The insects reportedly increased in size and might have been a species of frog.

Nearby, a building was scheduled for demolition with explosives. As the time drew near, traffic on the street was halted, and the building was cleared of people. The man reports running into a vacant but crowded building across the street with a female companion. The building was described as being set about fifteen feet higher, with low ceilings and few windows. When the adjacent structure was imploded, many in the crowd oohed and aahed, but the witness claims not to have seen it himself, as he was looking off to the left at that moment. Dust and rubble flew from the explosion in the form of concrete debris up to a foot in size, and the ground shook like in an earthquake. The man reported telling other onlookers "Look out; there's still more that might come."

Later in the day, as he was removing the water heater from the bathroom in his apartment, the man realized it was integrated into the bathtub, and was seriously old and rusted but surprisingly clean underneath. Below the tub, the floor was reportedly made of steel, and he could see down the drain. Of most concern, the witness alleges, was how he was going to be able to take hot showers or baths.

· · · · · ·

Dream job lacks supervision

Property owner disposes of formalwear

MIAMI — A man reportedly landed his "dream job" this week, explaining that the work was "self-directed" but "with no supervision." The work site, reportedly in a large sprawling house, had a sizeable television set, and the man reported watching television "to pass the time when the work was slow."

Later in the week, when returning to the work site in an all-terrain vehicle with his parents and two siblings, the man reported noticing a pile of garbage left at the curb by the owner of the house. He alleged that "it was all suits, in green and gray." The owner was reportedly standing at the gate, and turned out to be a beloved uncle. Even though several of the man's immediate relatives greeted him by name, the uncle acted as if he didn't recognize any of them.

· · · · · ·

Soap wrapper causes clog

LOCAL — While employed as a teacher at an area middle school, a man admitted today that he flushed the wrapper from a bar of soap down the oversize toilet. After the toilet clogged, the man allegedly poured acid in to unclog it. The school administrators reportedly assumed that "it was a plot orchestrated by some of the students."

· · · · · ·

Job interview involves lengthy swim

Floodwaters quickly recede

OTTAWA, CANADA — Returning to his former job at a bank in the city, a recently returned man stated that "I'm surprised they remembered me and actually gave me a job." The work environment was described as rife with "office politics."

Because the city's parks were flooded, the man reportedly swam in the Rideau Canal to get to his job interview, despite the fact that the parks reportedly dried up quickly. On arriving at the bank, the man was instructed to remain in the lobby for an interview. He explained that "I was surprised, but I don't actually know what's up."

Spa visit by bicycle

QUEBEC, CANADA — A visitor to a rural area in the province reported a lengthy but not unpleasant cycling trip to arrive at the spa town where a high school crush may or may not have been residing. "I had to cycle over a hill, then around a lake," the man explained. "It felt like the first day of

school: scary at first but fine once you understand it." Once at the spa, the man claimed he got undressed, and bathed, and lit some candles in his lit-tle wood-paneled room.

. . . . . .

Man questioned regarding residence

Tax collection unlikely

LOCAL — An area man reported that an individual asked him a question: "Do you live in that building?" When the witness replied in the affirmative, the man said, "That building is very hard to find." Although his identity remains unknown, the man is described as "moon-faced, with glasses." The witness stated that it seemed unlikely that the individual was a city tax official.

. . . . . .

Alleged trespassing on ship excursion

PACIFIC OCEAN — An area resident reports joining an excursion on a navy ship, despite the fact that "I was so incompetent with the work." The witness later revealed his motivation for the trip: "There was a hot guy I wanted to reconnect with." The targeted individual's job on the ship was described as "cutting things—he was a specialist in that." The man intentionally tied plastic to the ship's railings so that the cutting specialist would be summoned to cut it off. "I wound up in places I shouldn't have been," the witness explained, "including the captain's 1/45."

Authentic kitsch sought on escalator

LOCAL — This evening a local man introduced his childhood neighbors, a man and a woman and their son, to a dream researcher. The quintet enjoyed dinner, and the neighbor couple left, but then later came back. On their return, the witness alleges that "the woman had her underpants stuck in her butt crack." To reinforce the point that she was authentically kitsch without it being contrived, her husband reportedly stated that "Panties are not yet vindictive." When the couple took the down escalator ahead of the other members of the party, the woman fell onto her butt when stepping off the stairs. "She was embarrassed," the witness explained, "but since they'd been talking about vindictiveness, I told them, 'Neither are escalators.'"

Alpine eavesdropping reveals laundry mishap

NAGANO PREFECTURE, JAPAN — A visitor to an area forest amusement park reports looking down the mountain toward a farmhouse. Three people at the farm were allegedly forking hay into a horse pen. The man claimed he could hear their faint conversation, and one of the individuals reportedly said, "I bleached my jeans by mistake."

Bus trip inspections, bribes demanded

CD collection examined

TOKAI REGION, JAPAN — Riding as a passenger on a bus driven by an acquaintance, an area resident traveled in heavy traffic from the suburbs toward the city center. At a police checkpoint, the man's CDs were reportedly laid out and examined. One of the officers told the man that they would be returned to him, "but I wasn't completely clear on that, as she was speaking Japanese." When the bus stopped at a toll booth,

two women allegedly demanded a bribe to allow the bus to continue. The driver reportedly only had twelve tickets and thus refused to pay the bribe. Despite the lengthy hold-up, the bus was eventually allowed to proceed.

· · · · · ·

Medication distribution backfires

OUT WEST — Reportedly tasked with distributing candy laced with a medication to children in a village in a Native American nation, a man reports that the children didn't fall for the ruse, and instead threw it back at the interlopers. "We ate some as an example," the man claimed, "but they just weren't having it."

. . . . . .

Street pursuit and assault

TOKAI REGION, JAPAN — A local resident reported being stalked tonight by an RV containing a group of alleged "right-wing paramilitary guys." They pursued the witness, who was on foot, on a major boulevard, and attempted to stop him. Unsure of which direction to run—down the dark side street, or on the main street—the man reportedly hesitated, allowing four of the pursuers the opportunity to "jump out and grab me." The organization the men belonged to wasn't immediately identified. The man explains that "They weren't wearing uniforms, but I knew they were going to beat the shit out of me." This story will be updated as details become available.

. . . . . .

Sexual encounter interrupted by conference staff

Sky-blue lobby configuration "familiar"

MIDWEST — At a conference held this week in a local hotel and convention center, a visitor from out of state reported that the venue "wasn't dingy, just messy and hectic." The man reportedly shared a room with a man he didn't know, described as "blond and tall and a bit beefy, just a typical white Anglo type." The other attendee took the room's bed, and the witness slept nearby on a mattress on the floor. After they had said good night, the witness reported that he "got a weird vibe" when his roommate was sitting up in the bed, shirtless, watching him. The pair reportedly embraced, although the roommate "didn't want me to use much tongue when we were kissing." The pair reportedly had sex, with the witness stating that "I made sure it was a mutual thing."

The pair were interrupted when someone came in to talk to the witness. "I noticed then that our room wasn't private at all," the man explained. "It was directly connected to the hotel lobby." When the man walked to the front of the room, there were some tables arranged there in the darkness, and through an archway to the right was the hotel's lobby bar. People were reportedly hanging out there and quietly drinking and playing pool. On the left a staircase ascended from outside, and under the stairs the witness alleges that "I saw two kids in a bed in the alcove formed by the stairs." The man reported that the config-

uration looked familiar, adding "there's no wasted space." Upon questioning, the man elaborated that the beds themselves didn't look familiar, but rather the alcove itself did: "It was just a common template of a public space." The stairs and walls were reportedly painted a sky-blue color, with the hex color code #3EB7E3.

The man who had come to interrupt the witness during the sexual encounter was described as "kind of round-faced" with a mustache and round wire-rim glasses. His hair was light brown and "almost reddish, but not quite" mixed with gray. Described as "very polite," the man explained that he was working as a staffer for the conference event, and asked the witness, "We'd like to know if you'd be interested in helping out. We wondered if you could teach a group of small kids at the conference?" The witness reportedly demurred, stating that "I said I'd do it only if they were in a pinch, as I had taught kids before and didn't really enjoy it." At that point the witness explained that "I knew the blond guy and I were nev-er going to get any privacy from then on, so I looked back at him and gave him a meaningful look."

Rail yard incident, domestic disturbance on extended cross-country trip

Baggage racks overloaded

MANITOBA, CANADA — A visitor to the area reports that while on a cross-country car trip with two companions, in

Manitoba the group met a man who pointed out some scenic lakes and invited them to his home. At the residence, however, things took a dark turn when their host allegedly got into a physical altercation with his son. The son managed to overcome his father by flipping him over his back, but according to the witness, "I was the only one who saw it." The host allegedly expressed a desire to retrieve a knife from the garage, but the trio of visitors managed to calm him down, and soon left the residence.

The witness explained that "I assessed him as crazy," even though that came as a surprise to his travel companions. "I told them that his mental illness would always be the focus," the man explained. "Like being with a depressed person, that's always the main focus, the illness."

At some point the man separated from his travel companions and continued the journey on his own. He reported that "Every town is the same—the woods, and lots of water, and bandstands, and a right bend in the road."

Finding himself in a train yard, the man entered a nonpublic area and leaned against a wall.

At the train yard, he witnessed a passenger train with a steam locomotive break the track. Railroad employees reportedly proceeded to push the train backward, away from the broken section. The witness reported that he was unable to assist because "I had a bum leg," but stated that "the station guys helped me up the grade to get me out of the way." The witness speculated that the cause of the incident was that the train was extremely heavy, and traveling up the narrow grade damaged the tracks.

Aboard the train, the man reported searching for his belongings, and that once the train was underway again, "I realized it was nice to be on the road, even though I'd been traveling so long." Rejoined by one of his erstwhile travel companions, they found seats, and the man reportedly said, "Why is there never any room in the baggage racks?" His companion allegedly became angry and retorted that "Right there—there's room, right over there." The man responded, "All right; I don't want to hear it. It was a rhetorical question." He alleges that some international travelers sitting behind them, as well as a couple across the aisle on the right, "had too much stuff" and had filled the baggage racks.

Irresponsible firearm use

LOCAL — A man stated that he and a female friend were seated on a bench awaiting treatment for "a weird disease that everyone in the society has." The disease allegedly disrupted everything and "we were all sick." Another patient, described only as "a South African guy," sat with them on the bench. The trio eventually obtained the cure to the disease, at which point the South African allegedly picked up a revolver and playfully pointed it at the man's companion, pulling the trigger, but the weapon only clicked. The witness claims that "I warned him not to do it, because it was loaded." The South African subsequently aimed the weapon at someone to his right, pulling the trigger with a similar result. The third time, he aimed at the witness, and that time it fired a round. "I managed to catch the bullet casing in my hand," the witness explained, "but the bullet hit me, and the world went black, and I floated off somewhere else."

· · · · · ·

Red cubes required for movement

LOCAL — A man explained that there were two complementary individuals: one had eyes and other had eye sockets. When the red cubes were removed from the sockets, only gravel remained. The face was described as "huge" and "like a mask." The red cubes allegedly "make the truck run," the man explained, and were necessary for its movement.

Raucous wheelchair, bicycle trip in box canyon

Telephone use delayed

OUT WEST — A local man reported tonight that while using a wheelchair, along with an ex-boyfriend who was also using a chair, he incited public protests, rolling down a retail street and "causing hell." The man allegedly thrust a screwdriver into a cyclist's spokes, causing the man to lose stability but not to fall. The two vehicles reportedly become entangled, and the man was forced to slow down when the bicycle's spokes were caught in his wheels.

The man rolled into the adjacent canyon, on the west side of the commercial street. Described as a box canyon with high straight walls and one narrow entrance, it allegedly

still had water and mud in the bottom from recent rains. The man explained that the ground was uneven, there was no vegetation, and the rock walls were black, red, and gray. The witness and his ex traversed the length of the canyon, alternating between wheelchairs and ten-speed bicycles.

Later in the day, the witness described being "pissed off and vocal" about not being able to use a pay phone. There were long lines at the phone booths, and the man's ex was at the front of a line about thirty feet away. A woman reportedly asked the man for a quarter to use in one of the pay phones, and in exchange he took forty yen from her. The man admits that "I was getting too much money; I knew that." Additionally the woman gave him five one-yen coins "to make it more fair." When he used the phone, the man claimed that he couldn't reach whoever he was calling, reportedly an information number, and when he eventually did reach the number and obtain the information, he forgot it right away, and then complained about it.

Moving deeper into the canyon, the man described walking behind a low rough hill, where he sat down and saw a painting by an artist he was familiar with. "I realized it was a self-portrait," the man explained. The subject was described as "redhaired, but the painting wasn't very good, and it didn't look much like she did in real life." In an oblong frame, the left side of the artwork was described as a vivid painting of the artist from the neck up. "She had poofy American hair," the witness alleged. The right side of the painting was described as black, but with a mirror sketch of the face outlined in red paint.

At that point the man realized he needed to leave the canyon, as the rains had made landslides an imminent danger. He ran out quickly, aware that the canyon walls could slide on top of him at any moment. "They were rocky, and tall," the witness explained, "and I had to go right under them. Luckily I did escape."

Multiple arrests in shower melee

LOCAL — While using the men's locker room at his high school, an area man reported that the cleaning woman came in to work while he was still using the shower. A group of male students allegedly entered and "started to verbally harass me." In response the man threw soap at them, and the melee led to several arrests. "I got out through the restrooms," the man explains, "but the cops questioned me when I came back to get my bags." During the questioning, the man alleges that "I was accused of starting the whole thing." Eventually released, the man managed to barter with another student, who stood behind the rope cordon with some female students, to exchange bags.

• • • • • •

Father offers opium

LOCAL — Upon returning home tonight, a local man reportedly found his father smoking an unknown substance in a little dish using a straw. The parent claimed it was opium, and said, "You should give it a try." Not asking how the smoking process worked, the man attempted to smoke the substance but alleged that "I didn't get any" and instead only got a few bites of the straw, described as "sweet and crispy." When his father retired, the elder explained that "I have lots; go ahead and smoke." Left on his own, the witness was able to figure out how to burn the opium properly, and alleges that "I finally got enough to get buzzed."

• • • • • •

Breaking news

LOCAL — An unusual breaking news story was reported on cable television tonight. Describing the story, a local man claimed that it was "huge

CNN news" on multiple screens and involved a reference to Athens. Elements of the story allegedly included an appeal to "Come, we're in a world of many languages," although the witness admits that it might have been "a world of many landings." A secondary exhortation in the story was related as "Start to integrate."

. . . .

Boyfriend spotted from car

Hedge described as tea-like

THE COUNTRYSIDE — A local man described walking along a country road when a vehicle stopped and offered him a ride. The vehicle was a red Daihatsu Mira, driven by "a thin guy with dirty-blond hair." Once he climbed into the vehicle, the driver turned onto a main road, and they passed a man sloppily watering a hedge. "It looked like a tea bush," the man claimed, "but the leaves were too big for tea." Once they'd passed the man, the driver, described as "a bit geeky," said, "You know

that guy back there?" The witness stated that he realized then that it was the driver's boyfriend, and they exchanged a fist-bump.

Frenchwoman guided around national park

Driver "was me, and yet it wasn't me"

GATINEAU, CANADA — A visitor to the area reports that he was guiding a guest through the national park today in a car. "There was a driver," the man explained, "and it was me, and yet it wasn't me. I was him but he looked different than me, and I was somehow outside him." The principal passenger was described as a well-dressed foreign woman, possibly French, accompanied by one or two other passengers. The witness described some difficulty driving the car because it was equipped with hand controls for wheelchair users. "There was a handle to press both the brake and the gas." The man explained that "It was braking the car as I was driving, but I/ he figured it out, and I/he demonstrated the mechanism to the passengers."

Dogs mourned

LOCAL — An area man reported helping his uncle grieve over his recently deceased dogs. Walking around the neighborhood, the man stated that his uncle "paid his way" as an act of mentorship.

Family visit terminated early, earthquake ensues

THE COUNTRYSIDE — When an area man took his boyfriend to his parents' house to watch television, the man's mother allegedly used an antigay slur. The boyfriend pointedly kissed him, but the man stated that he was "angry, and just wanted to leave."

Later that day the man was on his own again, standing on a hilltop near the town, when he spotted his mother, brother, and sister-in-law drive past, allegedly headed to the hospital so that the younger woman could have a baby. He reportedly encountered the woman's mother, who was looking for them, when she attempted to telephone the hospital. "I didn't tell her I'd seen them," the man explained, "as I was looking for change to make my own call."

The man stated that he was in the phone booth when the earthquake hit. The booth was displaced from its moorings, nearby houses were knocked askew, and a fire broke out in a house directly across the street. The phone lines reportedly got busy as

"people were worried and freaking out."

• • • • • •

Nova Scotia road trip interrupted by hitchhiking stint

Man struggles to use thumb correctly

NOVA SCOTIA, CANADA — A man reported taking an RV trip with two college-era friends. Tasked with reading the map, the man sat in back while one of the women drove the RV, following a highway along the shore. "I was concerned that the RV would tip over," the man explained, as the driver was allegedly going too fast down a big hill, and there was a curve at the bottom. "I closed my eyes, but we survived," he stated.

Cities were visible in the distance, but the trio could not agree as to where they were on the map, or how far along they were in the journey. "The countryside seemed to pass quickly in comparison to the map," he stated, "but the driver said it wasn't fast enough for her."

At one point, when he

stepped out of the RV, the man lost track of the

vehicle. "We got separated," he explained, "and I had to hitchhike to our destination, where I assumed we would meet up again." Along the highway the man described standing in a place where there were other hitchhikers, described as "hippies." Assuming no one would stop, the man walked farther along the road. When a big truck passed him, he claims he held out "the wrong thumb, so it looked funny." The next vehicle that passed reportedly stopped for the hippies, and the subsequent one stopped for him.

The car was driven by a man described as "quite obese," and the front passenger was a woman who had recently had cosmetic surgery. In the backseat were their children. The witness reportedly sat in the front seat with the parents, and the man "drove very fast." Eventually they passed the RV, and the witness waved to his erstwhile traveling companions, but the couple in the car expressed confusion about what he was doing. When the driver pulled in at a highway rest stop, described as "positioned on a gentle incline," the family took a restroom break. When the man's traveling companions arrived at the rest stop, they departed together in the RV.

• • • • • •

Plumbing issue leads to embarrassment

LOCAL — A local man reported an embarrassing incident when a piece of plumbing equipment failed in the family bathroom. Even though the man was seated on the toilet, both his parents as well as two siblings entered the bathroom to discuss and troubleshoot the plumbing problem. Despite his entreaties for privacy, his immediate relatives allegedly "saw no reason to go." Seemingly unaware of his discomfort, the interlopers sat around the room to discuss the plumbing issue, and were reported to be "in good spirits."

• • • • • •

Pasta scheduled for dinner date

WEST HOLLYWOOD, CALIF. — A local man claims he recently made a dinner date in a restaurant with a tall, thin man. "He walked by and chatted me up," the man said, "and I'm going over there Thursday to teach him alfredo sauce." The agreement includes that the tall man prepare the pasta noodles. Further descriptions of the tall man include that he wears glasses, has short hair, and has a prominent forehead.

Pageant organizers cleared of homophobia

BIG BEAR LAKE, CALIF. — This mountain town was home to a series of beauty pageants organized by a group of men. They claim to have driven around the town in a station wagon for some time. One of the men reportedly expressed doubt as to whether another member of the group "could handle the gay thing," but the ringleader explained, "Of course he can, he's gay too." The vindicated homophobe was said to closely resemble a television character.

Phone line located next door

Empty office contains venetian blinds, potted fern

LOCAL — While walking in the downtown area, a local man reported that he attempted to telephone a local air conditioner factory to attempt to "get some psychic news" from the company answering machine. The man stated that his purpose was to formulate a mental puzzle for a friend, "because I knew he liked them." The man placed the call from a public phone on a main street and then heard a phone ringing in sync next door in an office. "I thought it couldn't be the same phone," the man claimed, and ended the call, but "it pre-guessed me": the neighboring phone stopped ringing a split second before he hung up. The man called back and realized that in fact it really was the same line. The phone was reportedly located in an empty ground-floor office with a big window, venetian blinds, and a potted fern, located in the adjacent building.

Unusual wildlife behavior on diving excursion

SANTA CATALINA, CALIF.—A Los Angeles man allegedly took a short boating trip with an aging Hollywood actor known for playing "tough guys." From a boat named *Treasure Island,* the pair reportedly made several scuba dives in occasionally murky water. At one point some black birds, similar to crows or ravens, became agitated and dropped dead, falling onto the boat, their bodies seriously damaged.

Reports came in that people in the vicinity had been "wooded"— completely overrun with stinging ants—so the pair employed a preventive method often used by the man's brother, rubbing vinegar on their faces and hands. The actor was reported to be quiet but not uncommunicative. "He wasn't around much," the witness explained, "and I was worried about diving alone."

Used Duo-Tangs for autobiography

LOS ANGELES — Several elderly Korean women assisted a man in creating a presentation about him in the Korean language. The document was presented in Duo-Tang binders and included photos of the man. The only problems were that the women were reportedly "a little hurried and careless" in preparing the document, and it was presented in used binders. The women also spent time gossiping about a Japanese woman that the man holds in high regard.

Family secrets revealed

CITY — A local man claimed that he was a guest at a dinner party held by his parents. He arrived in the rain, and while he was removing his rain gear, his mother allegedly pointed out to their other guests, "Look how tall he is," and subsequently compared his stature to his deceased uncle. More surprisingly, the man's father was alleged to have remarked in an off-hand manner, "His uncle was gay too."

Unknown *Gilligan's Island* episode uncovered

LOS ANGELES — A previously unknown episode of the perpetually rerun 1960s television program *Gilligan's Island* was uncovered today. In the episode, Gilligan is trying to get organized enough to go up in an industrial elevator. At the top is an unknown threat. As Gilligan prepares for his ascent, he is carrying a shotgun and a cup of coffee.

Pancake quest ends at rural market

Extended "sparse" journey by subway

CITY — A local man reported that a web design-

er, well known in the area and also connected to a TV chef, told him that a restaurant in another part of town was offering a 50-percent-off breakfast special. The restaurant was described as "up the road quite a ways," and she explained that the special was only available around 5 a.m. The man report-ed taking the subway "for several hours" to get there, but when he arrived, the special was already over. "I was there at the right time of day," he explained, "but the offer had expired." Not bothering to exit the subway, the man allegedly knew the offer had expired because there were no signs in the train or in the stations as he got near the restaurant, described as "like a Denny's."

The train subsequently went down a rural road where there was a stop at the end of a garden near a small pond. The stop was announced on the train as the stop for a new Seibu department store. "I didn't get off there," the man explained, "but continued on," eventually disembarking at a rural market just on the left side of the train.

The man claims that there was a middle-aged man, "a hippie type guy," on his right as he walked into the market. "I knew he was someone important or significant," the witness explained, "but I didn't stop to talk to him." The vendor was allegedly sitting on a stool selling postcards that depicted images of young children. "They were either photos or very realistic paintings," the witness claimed. "It made me uneasy, as I couldn't help but think 'pedophile.'" The children depicted were African, and the market was described as "either Southeast Asian or African."

Assessing his journey overall, the man explained that the day had a feeling of "sparseness": the interior of the train, the whitewashed city where the restaurant was located ("I just wanted pancakes"), and the barren market, where things were "few and far apart and not at all disorderly, the way nature is, but not cluttered the way a city or a market usually is." The man elaborated that the city and the market contrasted in feeling urban versus rural, and the color scheme was similarly white and cream in the urban area, and in browns and reds in the African market.

· · · · · ·

Group turns purple in UV light

LOCAL — Tonight an area man reported that he and three female companions "were doing weird things outside, near a chain-link fence." Their activities allegedly involved turning purple under UV light, a process that could cause

cars to crash, as well as becoming invisible.

Terrifying bridge climb

SAN FRANCISCO — A Los Angeles man visited the observation deck at the top of the Golden Gate Bridge along with his friend, a courier for a film production company. She explained that originally there had been only one tower to support the entire bridge, and that the second tower had been added later. The two were forced to climb down from the observation deck along the cable supports at the top of the bridge, an experience the man described as "terrifying."

• • • • • •

Sink repairs successful

MELROSE HEIGHTS, LOS ANGELES — The damaged restroom sink in the back of a shop in this commercial district has been repaired, reports say tonight. A friend of the shop's owners was able to repair a crack in the porcelain sink with a new kind of liquid porcelain crack filler.

• • • • • •

Clifford reexamined

LOS ANGELES — Clifford, the giant red dog of children's book fame, today reportedly became the focus of a demonstration of the nature of reality. Focusing on each part of Clifford—his eyes, his feet, his body—allegedly reveals their infinite potential to spin off on tangents of new ideas and new information.

• • • • • •

Stadium and cycling trips with renowned author

ELMIRA, N.Y. — Along with two other guides, a tour guide led a group of students to an event in a stadium and later on a cycling trip in upstate New York. Two of the guides had known a local author and psychic medium, and the group tried to interpret several artifacts from her life.

The lead tour guide forgot a personal item high in the stands of the stadium, and reportedly attempted to return to retrieve it after the event had finished. The man allegedly could not return all the way to where he had left the item, as the exit paths ended at the top. He reportedly remembered then that there had not really been a place for him in the stadium, and he had wandered around standing near people that he was acquainted with. To move to another part of the stadium, at one point he had had to climb through rooms that belonged to people who resided there. The man claims to have interrupted the ritual of one of the residents who appeared to have some psychological troubles; the ritual was described as "sad, crazy screaming." The guide passed through the room, assuring the resident that he would not be in the way of his ritual.

The group came across the medium beside the road in a ditch filled with golden grass. The lead guide reports having a sudden realization, and he said, "It's where your eyes have been." He showed the medium where to look through the viewfinder on her old bicycle, which provided a clear view of the distance. All of the members of the tour group reportedly wanted to look through the viewfinder.

A highway maintenance worker appeared agitated and asked the group to move out of the area, as he felt they were possibly damaging a structure that stood in the middle of the road. It was described as an old wooden structure with hardwood flooring that resembled a railroad carriage but was stationary.

Later the lead guide reports seeing the psychic's husband sitting at a cluttered round breakfast table. Although they did not speak, the man smiled and continued working on the psychic's financial paperwork, and reportedly called out to someone, "Bring that paper of mom's."

The lead tour guide

then returned to the stadium, where he claims he tried to find out what had been happening there earlier. The medium was waiting there at the front and knew what the guide was looking for. She allegedly explained something about herself that was connected to a small locket and a pink surface that was scraped away to reveal a mirror beneath that reflected her face. Previously she had buried something under a large tree. The guide reported that it was unclear whether it was a good thing or a bad thing, but that the item was protected by the roots and the building that stand on top of it now.

Boredom prompts movie walkout

PALM SPRINGS, CALIF. — A Los Angeles man reported going to the movies with his flight-attendant boyfriend today. They commented that the theater floor had an unusually steep rake sloping downward to the screen. Despite recent tensions in the relationship, the two allegedly sat together and "cuddled." In the row behind them sat an actor who had been seen on dates with the flight attendant, and the witness claimed that he felt very good that the flight attendant was out with him and not with the actor. Eventually the film became so boring that the pair walked out.

· · · · · ·

Studebaker eventually enters junkyard

LOS ANGELES — A local man reports repeatedly driving in and out of

the parking facility for his apartment building. The facility looked much like a junkyard. "The blue Studebaker was always behind me," he said, "and often missed the gate. It had to drive over the trigger pad again and again." Reports said the trigger pad to open the gate was in fact a tin badge from the car and had STUDEBAKER embossed on it. The man said he slid on the pad in order to allow the blue car into the junkyard.

• • • • • •

Shark food

CENTRAL JAPAN — Miniature sharks and other fish, each about 1.6 inches in length, formed the basis of a local resident's meal today. "They popped between my teeth like squid do," he explained. "It made me feel ill."

• • • • • •

Scanty outfit seen on Spring Street

DOWNTOWN LOS ANGELES — Visiting the Fashion District, a man reported this morning that he met the brother of a local designer and another man on Spring Street. Despite never having met the designer's brother before, and not engaging with the men in conversation, he claims that he knew immediately who it was. The brother's friend was described as tall and thin with messy hair, wearing a light beard, shorts, and a T-shirt. "He looked a lot like Shaggy from *Scooby-Doo*," the man reported. The designer's brother was dressed in a low-rise swimsuit, "aqua blue or tile blue, with a bit of white in the front." It was not immediately clear what the two men were doing in the Fashion District.

Minor mishaps on hotel first day

SAN FRANCISCO — A local man started a position as a hotel concierge, and reportedly needed to ask coworkers for assistance on some points of the job. His domestic partner, a short man with a disability in one arm, requested

that the man sign him up

for travel benefits with the hotel, which the man presented to his employers.

The hotel reportedly stands high on a hill that is served by cable cars. On his first day the man mistakenly carried a pile of dishes through the cable-car security check-point on his way to the concierge desk. On the same day he received a note from a room in the hotel that had a broken ceiling lamp hook; another note requested police protection for a night march through a public park in a city in Japan.

Radiator mix-up

TOKAI REGION, JAPAN — An area resident reported parking his car outside a garage in a coastal city today, only to find on his return that the mechanics had removed the radiator and left the establishment to buy a radiator hose. A colleague of the man's from Los Angeles was at the garage and knew some of the older mechanics who were still on the premises. Because she allegedly spoke Japanese, the man requested that she explain to the mechanics that "I didn't really want this, and I need my car."

Shoplifting incident

MELROSE HEIGHTS, LOS ANGELES — A West Hollywood man and several friends were left in charge of a local store today. A young man and an older man, both wearing trench coats, entered the store, and the store minder witnessed the younger man steal a gem-encrusted dog bone–shaped piece of jewelry inscribed with the word T-BONE. As they were walking out the door, the store minder took the thief's arm and said, "There was a piece of jewelry."

The thief handed over the item and surrendered his driver's license, which the store minder took into the back to photocopy. While he was making the copy, the two men stole four other items, including a large flower-print handbag. The store minder reports that he told the thieves, "We've already prosecuted three people." The thieves left the store, and the store minder called after them, "Don't show your faces here again." The thieves allegedly responded with derisive laughter, to which the store minder reiterated, "I'm not kidding; don't come back." The man claims that at that point, the thieves stopped laughing.

• • • • • •

Kmart remembered

LOS ANGELES — Past advertising by discount retailer Kmart was remembered today with a new campaign using the slogan "See the plaid that made us famous." The campaign juxtaposes images of the Kmart marquee as it was in 1969, news of the Stonewall riots ("Gay Uprising in New York"), and old advertising ("Plaid Pants $2.99").

At the same time, another department store unveiled its own alternative clothing aisle. In addition to traditional clothes, the aisle displayed a variety of glittery drag wear.

• • • • • •

New arts center designed

LOS ANGELES — Architects began work on a local arts center and museum today. Initial designs for the building include a tall white structure at the back and a lower red-and-black rounded building in the front. The front building was designed as administrative offices with red pillars on the inside, similar to Japanese public buildings. It would reportedly also contain gardens. Critics of the project commented that the designs "look like a giant toilet."

Man takes up smoking

WEST HOLLYWOOD, CALIF. — A local resident reports taking up smoking for the first time at age thirty-eight. "I assume that I won't get addicted, as long

as I just smoke a little," the man stated. While perched on the concrete steps in front of a city apartment building, he described in detail the tactile sensation of rolling a cigarette between his fingers and gently inhaling smoke. "I wasn't doing it to be cool, because none of my friends were there," he claimed.

. . . .

Dead body in toilet cubicle

Feet visible from next stall

MEXICO — While visiting a local theme park, a man reported today that he realized there was a dead body in the next toilet stall in the men's room. The man stated that "I could see the feet" and that he hoped no one would notice the body and blame him, because "I didn't do it." In the stall the man was allegedly cleaning off his kitchen knife with toilet paper, explaining that he was removing "dark-red rust." He stated that he left the men's room "carefully" in the hope that no one saw him.

Baked earth potential

SONORAN DESERT, CALIF. — Cracked, baked earth in a dry lakebed came under scrutiny today. Brownish-yellow in color, it was reported to be vibrating like buzzing bees, ready to spring to life or morph into something else and move on.

Boot incident on bus

Passengers sleep, try on shoes

MONTREAL — A visitor to the city reports riding on the rear bench seat of a city bus. Many of the other passengers were sleeping, and several had taken off their shoes, leaving them on the floor. Passengers who were not sleeping were trying on the shoes. The visitor claims to have tried on a pair of new black boots. A passenger on the bus dressed in a black brushed-wool winter jacket, sporting a medium-length wavy dark haircut, reportedly woke up, followed by a woman, who asked where her boots were. The visitor reports that at that point, he surreptitiously removed the boots.

Mobile phone destroyed

LOS ANGELES—A local man reported tonight that he discovered his cell phone "completely smashed up" with springs and a "wacky dial" coming out of it. The man described the effect as "something like a 1940s cartoon."

. . . . . .

Old rival lectures in airport

Paperwork completed

CALGARY, CANADA — In the departure lounge at the airport here, a traveler waiting to catch a flight allegedly heard a woman's voice in an adjacent partitioned area. "It was an unusual voice," the traveler claimed, "and at first I didn't know who it was." He realized that she was addressing him personally, and the content of her monologue allegedly involved a criticism of the traveler for having left his hometown. Realizing it might be a certain junior high school rival, he walked behind the partition to find that his suspicions were correct. He continued working on the papers that he carried, and she allegedly continued her talk despite the fact that he was standing right in front of her.

When he finished his paperwork, he stepped closer to confront the former rival. "I don't remember what I said," he explained. "I didn't convince her of anything, but she didn't get any more agitated either. I was proud of my restraint."

Man grows mustache

WEST HOLLYWOOD, CALIF. — Reports indicate that a local man has grown a mustache. "I've never liked them," he admitted, "but I looked in the mirror and it kind of made me look hot," in a manner reminiscent of the 1970s.

• • • • • •

Cold War–style disaster at airport

LOS ANGELES — On a flight on final approach to LAX, a local man returning from vacation with his father reportedly noticed several fires burning in the city and in the hills. "There were fat columns of thick black smoke," he claimed. As the plane banked to the right and descended along the hillside, the man allegedly caught a glimpse of "a huge mushroom cloud" on the other side of the hills. He closed his eyes and braced himself in his seat, hoping the plane might survive, but he realized that was impossible, and felt the plane being vaporized in the blast.

Zombie attacks rage on two planets

PLANET MARS AND INTERPLANETARY SPACE — Zombies attacked a working spaceship on Mars, reports from the red planet said today. The twenty crew members claim that the zombies "were coming out of hills, massing all around the ship" and eventually entered it. They alleged that the only way to kill the zombies is with a bullet to the third-eye area of the forehead or by "splashing them with water." Humans venturing out on the surface of Mars were reported to be carrying glasses of water with them everywhere they went.

"It must have been something in the Martian soil," an expert stated, "because these people had been human and turned into zombies after walking around on Mars." Zombie attacks were also reported in interplanetary space on ships plying the Mars–Earth route, and there were some indications that zombies had attacked in the Arizona desert on the home planet.

One eyewitness reported that it was impossible to tell the difference between normal humans and zombies because they looked the same. "But the zombies move close to you, to try and infect you," he claimed. "If they touch you, you're infected." The man reported splashing many individuals who "came too close" with his glass of water, both on Mars and on interplanetary ships. He also reported constantly refilling his water glass from available fountains and sinks. Often they were just humans but occasionally, he alleges, they were zombies and melted from the water. "On one of the spaceships I saw Captain Kirk from the original *Star Trek* series," the man alleged. "I'm still not sure if he was human or zombie, because he didn't say anything."

Diving photo disputed

Pool users "lethargic"

LOS ANGELES — A local man reports sensing unspoken hostility in a local swimming pool. "It might have been because I'm out and they are all straight," he suggested, "or because they're still holding some grudges from high school days." The pool-goers were said to be using the diving board in a lethargic way, simply walking off the end of it into the water in-

stead of getting any spring in their steps. Individuals lined up on the board three or four at a time.

Finally the man requested that they clear the board so that he could get some height on his dive. A colleague from grade school, now a sports promoter, wanted to take a photo of the dive for later publication in the news media, but the man claims that he "knew it would be embarrassing." The sports promoter waited at the bottom of the pool, clad in yellow swim trunks, and the man refused to dive until he moved out of the way. "He was right where I was going to dive," the man said.

After completing the dive, the man discovered that another grade-school colleague had taken an amateur photo of the dive while in the water. The man discovered the camera in the pool and claims he let water into the battery compartment of the camera's flash unit in order to disable it. The amateur photographer still had the film, however.

The man pursued the duo to a newspaper office, where it was discovered that the sports promoter was actually a professional photographer. Unable to determine whether a photo had been taken of the dive, the man eventually found a roll of film from the amateur photographer's camera. As the man was about to open the roll of film and expose it to light in order to destroy it, the sports promoter intervened, pleading that there were other images of value on the roll of film. The man hesitated, not exposing the film, and the sports promoter reportedly said, "I never should have bought you that puppy that time. You didn't want it." He went on to explain that he had purchased the animal because he had "always loved you as a friend, but you just don't get it." The man claims he decided then not to expose the film.

India partitioned yet again

NEW DELHI — India has reportedly been partitioned again, although the name of the newly created state has not been determined. "The north is still called India," a witness stated, but below the curving border, which runs latitudinally across the middle of the subcontinent in a "happy face" shape, the name of the newly created state is not clear. Witnesses pored over maps in an attempt to determine what city the new state had been named after, and despite a minority consensus that it "might be Bangalore," no clear determination has been made.

Supermarket high jinks lead to car chase

Woman morphs into man

LOCAL — Reportedly out grocery shopping with a childhood friend tonight, a local man alleged that his companion purposely fell down next to her grocery cart near the checkout "only for a laugh."

The man then did the same thing, much to the reported amusement of his companion. The woman staffing the checkout station sternly criticized their actions, and allegedly "gave her hell." The man asked to see the manager, who was equally nonplussed, and the pair then "ran away."

His female companion became a man from a later period in his life, and the pair allegedly chased other vehicles in a car. Eventually spotting a roadblock up ahead, the two men sought another supermarket to escape into.

· · · · · ·

Tornado touches down in central LA

LOS ANGELES — Witnesses report that a waterspout or similar tornado-like cloud touched down in central Los Angeles during the recent storms. "It seems like it would have hit somewhere around Los Angeles City Hall," one witness said, "but it might have been closer to us in the Larchmont neighborhood."

· · · · · ·

Man wakes to find self in bed

WEST HOLLYWOOD, CALIF. — A local man reported waking during the night to be confronted with a sleeping version of himself. "He looked blue in the darkness, and his mouth was lolling open. He was clearly asleep," the man claimed. "The scary part was that when I tried to rouse him, he wouldn't wake up. I didn't know if he was dead or what." Asked if it was perhaps his doppelgänger, the man stated that he believed that "it was more like a parallel version of me. I had the sense that there were other mirror-image people around too, but they weren't in the room with me." Analysis of the incident continues.

· · · · · ·

Albino rodent explores garage

Found wearing harness and leash

LOCAL — Late yesterday afternoon a former area resident reports finding an albino rodent—"It could have been a thin rat, or a chubby stoat," he claimed—with a harness around its midriff and a leash attached. It's coloring was "pinky and off-white, like he'd been playing in the dirt a lot." The man claims to have taken the leash and walked the animal around the ex-  terior of his father's garage. "There's all sorts of stuff stored there," he explained, "and the little guy was digging around in it." Unlike a domestic animal, however, the man reported that the animal was "jumpy" and "tugged on the leash as if I wasn't even there."

Envelopes mislabeled
Deliverability still unclear

WEST HOLLYWOOD, CALIF. — A local man reports placing labels on an envelope in the wrong places. "I always put the green label to the left of the shipping label," he claimed, "but for some reason I switched them around." At press time there was no word as to whether the mix-up would affect the deliverability of the envelope in the postal system.

Docile celebrity-adjacent zombie spotted
LA zombie "wandering"

LOS ANGELES — The brother of a television actor was seen roaming the West Hollywood neighborhood late last night, having been transformed into a zombie. "He had those electric-blue zombie eyes," one witness reported, "but he was totally not dangerous or trying to attack anyone; he was just wandering around."

. . . . . .

Man buys muscle car
Had talked about a hybrid

LOS ANGELES — A local man came home with a classic Chevy Malibu muscle car, "souped up with the chrome wheels and everything," his roommate claimed. The man had allegedly talked about buying "one of those hybrids" because of environmental concerns, "but I guess he wanted the heavy acceleration instead." Neighbors who were witness to the incident report that the man showed off the "new" car by revving the engine.

. . . . . .

Moisturizer bleaches hair
Man goes blond by accident

WEST HOLLYWOOD, CALIF. — Sporting a frosted-blond look for the first time, a local man explained that the moisturizer he was using on his face had caused his normally dark hair to change color. "I probably ran my hands through my hair with it," he claimed.

. . . . . .

Mountain bus trip leads to bedroom
Excursions marred by ATM problems, waterslide nudity

LOS ANGELES — Two Miracle Mile residents reported catching the bus into the mountains several times today. Before one of the excursions, the two had coffee at an outdoor café at the corner of Fairfax Avenue and Beverly Boulevard. When the bus was seen approaching, they could not locate the server in the crowded interior of the café, so the man left a $10 bill on the table. "We weren't sure if $10 would cover what we had—two slices of pie, a coffee, and a beer—but I thought it was close, and that we could check back the next time, on the way home."

The woman allegedly ran across the street to catch the bus, headed west on Beverly into the mountains, while the man left the money. She reportedly boarded the bus while the man ran across the street ("I didn't think she would," he explained). The bus started to creep along the curb as the man approached the door, and he had to jump aboard as it was moving.

On another of the trips, this one in the evening, the pair reportedly ran into an acquaintance and her physically disabled son, Timmy, who were already aboard. On boarding the bus, the bus driver allegedly stated that he could not carry Timmy from the bus to his house in the mountains, but the passengers knew it would not be a problem. "We had an alternate plan for once we got up there," the man explained. The driver also informed passengers that it was raining in the mountains ahead but that there were clear patches, and he could not be sure if it would be raining at their destination or not.

On their third trip, the man attempted to withdraw money from an ATM, but was allegedly refused because he had only twelve dollars in his account. "The ATM was squat and wide like those cigarette machines from the 1970s," he explained. The man's debit card slid into an open space in the machine rather than into the card-reading slot, and fell through the machine to the floor below. "I had to reach under and fish it out," he claimed.

Upon arriving in the mountains, the man encountered an old friend from Tokyo who runs a graphic design business, and the two went down the waterslide together. The slide was several miles long and made of granite. "It was square-shaped, like a sluice," the man explained. They floated on black stone slabs that were shaped like paddleboards. Other people were also playing in the water, including the facility's hosts, two identical twins who bore an uncanny resemblance to the man's college roommates but were in fact not them. The man and his Tokyo friend reportedly rode the slide all the way to the bottom, where there were no other people. The Japanese friend "was a bit embarrassed because I rode down totally naked," the man explained.

The Japanese man's house was at the bottom of the slide, and the pair allegedly entered his parents' bedroom. It was octagonal with curtained windows on six of the sides. A large canopied bed stood in the middle of the room, and out the left windows were the entrance stairs to the house, whose front door was just outside the bedroom. The room's curtains and canopy were reportedly thin transparent muslin, "yards of it," which the man explained was "billowy and light and bright in the sunlight streaming in from outside." The color of the muslin was described as very faint, "between pink and peach."

The Japanese man was nearly naked as well, and the man claims that he got the feeling he wanted to make out or have sex, "although I hadn't planned on that at all." The Japanese man was concerned that his parents might arrive home at any moment, and sure enough they did—the pair claim they saw them walking up the stairs outside the house.

The man wanted to turn the lights on for them, so the pair fiddled with the light switches on the wall near the bedroom door opposite the windows. "I had a tiny Philips screwdriver and was adjusting the screws on the face plate of the switch box," the man explained. At the

same time his friend repeatedly flipped the three horizontal switches. Finally he found the right combination of switches, and the lights outside came on.

Psychologist seduces patient

Home seduction turns into orgy

LOS ANGELES — Reports tonight indicate that a local man was seduced by his psychologist. The two were in session at the psychologists home when "he just kind of kissed me, and we went for it," the man reported. "I was wonder- ing why it was so dark in there, and why he was talking in such a distracted way. Then he's leaning over me, and sure enough that's what he was after." The man also reported that other men appeared in the room as things "got more involved." "I would roll over and there would be another naked guy there," he claimed.

The man reported returning to the home where the incident occurred later that night "to have a look around." He explained that the home had narrow passageways and a lot of "dark polished wood, like mahogany. It was on dry land in the middle of town, but it felt like being on a boat."

Toy plane strikes tanker truck

Leak but no explosion of mystery liquid

LOS ANGELES — Reports indicate a tanker truck was struck by a miniature airplane, piercing the hull near the upper rear of the vehicle and releasing some of the unidentified liq-uid contents. "The plane was only about six inches wide," a witness said, "and the stuff was leaking out quite slowly. We were just happy it didn't explode."

• • • • • •

Duck head becomes political boss

Kept in cherrywood cabinet

OUT WEST — Sources reported this evening that a disembodied duck's head has been put in charge of political affairs in the planet's western hemisphere. "It's awake and aware, and its eyes move around, but it mostly lies on its side and doesn't say anything," an anonymous source explained. The head is reportedly kept on a shelf in a nice cherrywood wardrobe at an undisclosed location. The doors of the wardrobe are left ajar to allow air to circulate freely.

Lawyer refuses estate disbursement

Dining set described as "huge" and "cool"

LOS ANGELES — Attempting to execute the estate of a woman he claimed was named "J. C. or J. D.," a local man claimed today that he tried to contact a lawyer named Frank who works at a Los Angeles–based publishing company in order to turn over custody of a dining-room table described as "huge" along with the "very cool collapsing pine chairs." The furniture had been unloaded at the train station, and the lawyer reportedly would not take calls from the executor. "I did speak to his colleague on the phone," the man admitted, "but his voice was so faint I could hardly hear him."

Man trapped by wild animals

"Nasty critters" give chase

WEST HOLLYWOOD, CALIF. — Wolves, wild boars, and what is being described as "other nasty critters" pursued a local man this evening, eventually trapping him on a stack of pallets in the corner of a room. The man, obviously in distress, called out for help. The incident is still being investigated.

Successful maiden flights end in tragedy

WESTERN EUROPE — Two Concorde-like experimental space planes made their maiden flight today with a large group of individuals from the same high school on board. Both planes arrived safely at their destination, despite comments by a woman acting as flight attendant that there was the smell of fuel and fuel residue inside the fridge on one of the planes.

Two passengers on the plane allegedly waited on

the tarmac for the second plane to arrive, but they were forced to remain sitting on the concrete apron until the second plane pulled up and stopped. As the two men and the acting flight attendant walked toward the hangar, an individual higher up in the space-plane program reportedly shouted at them to run inside. They were walking beside the plane, and its windows had visibly begun to ice up. The three managed to run into the hangar to safety before the plane exploded, but the director of the program and many others perished.

• • • • • •

Full-room tie-dyeing technique

TORONTO — Sources report that a local comedian was seen using a unique tie-dyeing system set up in a suburban home. Witnesses said the floor of the living room in the house was built on a twenty-degree slope with uneven surfaces and obstacles intrinsic in the design. Various streams of dye are pumped from the higher end of the room in large quantities.

On the day in question, the comedian and other participants, wearing the garments to be dyed, reportedly rolled and slid around on the sloping floor in what witnesses called a fairly effective method of dyeing the fabrics.

Unexpected return to Japan

Snacks, beer purchased

TOKYO — Many years since leaving the country, a former resident claims that he found himself back in Tokyo today. "I ordered *sembé* rice crackers and beer from a market stall on a crowded street," the man reported.

• • • • • •

Good hot spring sought

Tahitian springs prove disappointing

TAHASIA HOT SPRINGS — Speaking with a female friend from high school, a Los Angeles man attempted to uncover the name of a hot spring the two had visited in the past. "I asked her what the name of that great hot spring she took me to was," he claimed.

The woman allegedly told him it was called Tahasia.

"I tried to go once," the man explains, "but I thought it was in Tahiti." He further describes the hot springs in Tahiti as "disappointing." The pair eventually went to Tahasia hot springs, which the man claims to have found relaxing.

Crocodile hatchlings responsible for wider cosmological symmetry

Actor lookalike implicated in maintaining space-time

UNKNOWN LOCATION — Crocodile hatchlings play an invaluable role in maintaining symmetry in the universe, sources reported this evening. "It's an extension of cosmology, really," a scientist involved with the revelation stated. The recent discoveries include a long, darkened hallway in an underground location with an open stone tank at one end. One or more crocodiles in a state of hibernation inhabit the tank, described as being about three feet high and six by ten feet long and wide.

A woman wearing a dark-red cloak reportedly slowly wanders the hall, purportedly helping to maintain "cosmological balance." Although the woman's name is not currently known, scientists close to the discovery report that she bears a resemblance to a television actor who gained fame in the 2000s. Although few details are known at this time, part of the woman's role seems to be exchanging crocodile hatchlings from an exterior, unknown location into the tank. "The crocs aren't dangerous when they're in the tank," the source explained, "only during the exchange of the hatchlings."

Other details, such as the rumor that the hatchlings are transported in a shrunken, suspended state between the woman's toes, could not be corroborated. The scientist admitted that "we really don't understand everything about this installation yet. All I can say for sure is that the existence of this hallway and the crocodile tank, and the woman's work there, are responsible on the subatomic level for keeping the fundamental constituent particles of matter and energy from annihilating each other. On the cosmological level, this place and her work are responsible for keeping our familiar four-dimensional space-time from collapsing in on itself."

Pop stars "not stuck-up at all"
Details of bizarre makeover

LOS ANGELES — An area resident reports today that after "hanging out" with a famous pop singer and her sister, the pair are "not stuck-up at all." The only unusual thing, the main claimed, is that the younger sister allegedly had a complete makeover and cosmetic surgery so that she looked exactly like her sister. "It was like they were twins," the man stated. "I couldn't tell them apart. They were even wearing the same pink dress."

· · · · · · ·

Man requested to remove bicycle helmet
Helmet, glasses unacceptable in electronics store

LOS ANGELES — A local man claims that he was asked to remove his bicycle helmet and sunglasses while browsing at a newly opened electronics superstore in the city. "The guy was fairly polite," the man explained. "And he let me keep my earphones on. I guess it was some kind of security issue." Store officials could not be reached for comment at press time.

Confusing pole dance

Youth requested to perform by grandparents

LOCAL — A former area resident reported he was shocked when his parents requested that his twelve-year-old niece perform "a pole dance" for them. "I told them it wasn't appropriate for someone that age," he claimed, but "they insisted that she do it."

When the youngster eventually performed the dance, he realized it was in fact a maypole dance, which he agrees is something that is age-appropriate for a child. "I was just freaked out that they were trying to make a twelve-year-old dance like a stripper," he explained. "But in reality they weren't."

Hot-spring mukluk incident

Boot soaked; friend surprisingly "erudite"

SIERRA SPRINGS, CALIF. — A Los Angeles man reported tonight that he visited the local hot springs with a friend from Berkeley, Calif., and her daughter. "The place seemed to be mostly crowded with gay couples," he alleged. While they were bathing in the hot pools, he claims the Berkeley woman then gave him her boots, a pair of mukluks, to put in a dry place; one boot "fell in the water" but the man reportedly then dried it out with his towel.

A friend of the man

from high school, whom he had not seen since that time, was also in the water, and allegedly had a lively discussion with the Berkeley woman. "Unlike in the past," the man explained, "she was upbeat, erudite, and had extremely clean teeth."

· · · · · ·

Secret Velveeta code decrypted

LOS ANGELES — A can of Velveeta cheese was discovered beside a swimming pool today, with the name and address of the finder's friend in Philadelphia written on it. "I realized it might be in code so that no one could intercept it," the finder stated. The contents of the encoded message? An explanation of where the Philadelphia man's missing car was.

Man meets blue god

Charged with symbolic tasks

BUDAPEST — A Los Angeles–based visitor to the city claims he met "a blue god" that rose up sixteen feet out of the hot water in the bathtub in his hotel room. The god then allegedly proceeded to present him with three symbolic tasks. "It was a little freaky at first," he explained, "but after he was standing there, I wasn't scared." When asked about the shade of blue, the man explained "He was quite dark, a kind of shiny royal blue, or a dark indigo."

When questioned about the tasks he was allegedly given, the man explained that the first involved "pouring a mug of very hot water on a hilltop in the countryside near where I grew up," the second involved "driving around the countryside," and the third "I can't remember."

· · · · · ·

Vicious mafia hit on train

Mafiosi, victim mystified at brutal shooting

LOS ANGELES — On a train carriage that backed out of an underground shed, a local man reported tonight that he was with two older mafiosi, "not really friends, but I knew who they were." The man claimed that "we were almost safe then," except for a young former soldier wearing a blue shirt. "I was sitting behind him, and I shot him in the head, and then walked farther back in the train car." The older mafiosi were reportedly not upset, but were heard to say, "Look what he did. Why did he do that?"

The victim did not expire, so the shooter claims that he then disembarked from the train. "It was moving slowly," he alleged, "and I was at the right rear corner. The guy I shot came to the window. He wasn't angry, although his head was bleeding a bit. He asked me, 'Why'd you do that?'" At this point the shooter claims that he reloaded his gun and shot the victim several times in the head. "My gun was more like a cell phone, and it made a soft buzzing sound when I fired," he claimed.

The victim was allegedly still talking to the shooter and attempted to grab his ammunition magazine. "He still wasn't angry, and I shot him several times through the shirt, aiming for the heart." The victim is reported to have said, "Why did you have to do that?" The shooter claimed that the victim bled "quite a lot" but that because it was raining, the blood mostly washed away. The train stopped moving at that point, and the shooter moved off down the track.

Draft letter must suffice

Classmates help draft letter in Mandarin

LOS ANGELES — At the request of a local man, two Chinese nationals assisted a classmate in drafting a letter in Mandarin. "I had to go home and make a decision about whether to pursue it or not," the man alleged. "Once I had made the decision, I went back to talk to my classmates." The two men reportedly assured the letter writer that they would write a complete version of the letter later, and forward it to him by mail. "I knew that was unlikely," the man claimed, "but I had a very brief version of the letter in broken Chinese, so I knew I'd have to use that."

• • • • • •

Mission planned

LOS ANGELES — Three men planning a very positive mission were seen on a break from their planning work today, sitting on a sofa. All three men resembled very ordinary and average people, and all three wore blue polo shirts.

Fugitive evades police with elaborate tale

Detective interviews at LAX, suspect apartment

LOS ANGELES — Several days ago a man reported joking with a female acquaintance about his non-existent fiancée. When it became clear that the police were looking for the woman, the pair agreed to switch her identity to one of the man's female friends and pose as his fiancée. The man stated that "we fooled the police."

In a hallway at the airport, a police detective questioned the man about his fiancée's sister. When he saw that the fugitive woman was also present, he allegedly gave the detective the fake names the pair had used previously.

The detective looked at the fugitive woman and said, "Wait—that's your name."

The man reportedly then feigned surprise, raising his eyebrows and stating, "Oh, you're her sister." The police detective then accompanied the pair to the witness's apartment, where he had a moment alone with the fugitive woman to discuss the situation. The woman removed her red-haired wig to adjust it, and the man claims he proposed that they tell the police detective that his fiancée had died in a car crash around the time the fugitive woman had left the country. The woman allegedly stated that she believed they had to tell the detective that the fiancée was still alive, but "out of town."

The police detective, a woman with short blond hair, was clearly suspicious of the story and tried to uncover the truth with a series of "aha" statements. The man claimed that he was able to "fool" her by showing her the various parts of his apartment: the large classroom where he and a high school–era friend taught; the water room, which currently only had pools in it but which could be converted into a wet garden; and the upstairs, with the man's bedroom and the attic.

The man and the fugitive, along with the detective, lined up outside the attic with their luggage carts, behind "dozens of other people and their kids" who were waiting for a chance to store their luggage and their toys in the attic.

· · · · · ·

Renovations done with telekinesis

Group redesigns building with mental power alone

LOS ANGELES — A small group of individuals atop a local apartment building reportedly redesigned the building using only the power of their minds. "We were trying to figure out where the best place for the staircase would be going down into the apartments," one participant reported, "and when I imagined it in a new position, it would be there."

Other people in the group were working on different parts of the building, repositioning physical objects simply by imagining them in a different place. "One guy was older, with salt-and-pepper hair," the participant reported, "and there was also this hippie woman with blond hair." Asked to describe the redesign technique in more detail, the man stated, "It's like designing something on a computer as compared to designing it on a drafting board; it's instant, and effortless."

Massive snake attack

Reptiles bite and don't let go

WEST HOLLYWOOD, CALIF. — A local man reported tonight being bitten by many snakes. "They bit in with their fangs and hung off my face and hands," the traumatized victim stated.

Driving, parking incident in Japan

Trip ends on fashionable street

TOKAI REGION, JAPAN — Reports tonight indicated that a former resident returned to Japan for the first time in several years. He allegedly went driving with an old friend on the underground freeway that encircles a city park. "I wanted to stop by my old apartment," the man claimed, but they parked the car inside a shop on a fashionable boulevard.

Invigorating board game

PHILADELPHIA — A visitor to the city reported playing a board game with a college acquaintance. Described as resembling go, "with black and white pieces," the witness explained that he felt energized by the acquaintance.

Return to Accra

Minor hospitalization, Polish visitors mark trip

ACCRA, GHANA — After an absence of many years, a man returned to Accra this week and claims to have "walked around in bare feet, following my old routes." The central market was muddy, he explained, and he waited there for something, "but I wasn't impatient." Although he was not ill, the man was hospitalized "for tests or something."

The hospital room allegedly had two beds positioned at different angles, "like a dorm room," and at one point the man claims that a group of Poles, "all older people," came in and sat around the room, talking loudly. The man was reportedly attempting to conduct a phone conversation with a woman friend, another Westerner who lived in Accra, "but it was too difficult to understand her accent on the phone, and anyway she spoke too softly." He then reportedly ended the call and attempted to converse with the Poles. A nurse arrived to discharge the man while an elderly Polish man was being admitted. "So I packed up my newspapers and went home to read them and check my email."

Blond man appears as partridge

Hops away from pouncing tiger

WEST HOLLYWOOD, CALIF. — A blond man reportedly appears as a partridge in order to fly away from a tiger each time the beast pounced, reports tonight indicate. "He's playing a game with the tiger," a source familiar with the ongoing incident stated.

Confusing attempt to board subway

Station, system described as "dark," "industrial," "hexagonal"

LOS ANGELES — A local man attempted to board the subway this evening but described the station as "this vast symmetrical descending structure

with ramps and gates going down toward the center." He also described it as reminiscent of an arena, and alleges that "there were four different directions you could go, but the maps and gates were not well labeled. I just didn't want to miss the train."

Major revisions in legal jargon

Latin term replaced with modern English

WASHINGTON, D.C. — Information came to light today that indicates the legal term *habeas corpus* will soon be replaced with the phrase *habeas buttocks*. No explanation was immediately available for the revision, and observers emphasized that this was not to be interpreted as a humorous turn of events.

Miss Piggy found to be queen of the Earth

Man forced to dance to funky music

PLANET EARTH — After a brief absence from the planet, a man reportedly visited a shopping mall and ran into his father. The two decided to leave the mall because a group of women there "were having a dress party." The men went down to the street, at which time the man's father explained that Miss Piggy had become the despotic queen of the Earth. In disbelief the man viewed the pits and trenches where the poor were kept under guard on Miss Piggy's orders. "It still seemed like Earth," the man explained, "but something had happened while I was away."

Later the man was driving with friends in a van when he claims that "we were treated like pawns." The group was allegedly told to walk out on a board suspended over a lake, and the board was subsequently shaken. A New York City–based magazine editor known to the man appeared on the scene, at which point he realized the editor was somehow involved in administering the Miss Piggy regime.

Eventually the man was taken to Miss Piggy's chamber, where "she forced me to dance to funky music." The man reported that he was able to escape because "a man who looked just like" 1960s *Beverly Hillbillies* television actor Buddy Ebsen allegedly crashed a bright-red three-quarter-ton truck just outside as a diversion.

· · · · · ·

Man seeks own front door

Medicine vials appear on neighbor's step

SOUTH LOS ANGELES — Leaving his house earlier today, a local man realized two of his medication vials had been pulled from the trash, refilled with water, and displayed prominently on a neighbor's step. Attempting to return to his own residence, the man reportedly walked into a different neighbor's house and realized the unknown photos and unusual wall colors were not his own. He tried a second door with a similar result before finally finding his own front door.

· · · · · ·

Confusing gas burners heat up leftovers

Burners turned off without incident

SOUTH PASADENA, CALIF. — A local man reported heating up leftovers in the company of a police officer who had played on the man's C-league baseball team. "He was reheating turkey and other stuff," the man alleges, "and he had put a ceramic plate under the burner." The faint blue flames licking

up around the plate "were startling" but "it looked

safe enough."

When they were finished reheating the food, the man claimed to have turned off the burners, as well as turning off burners on other stoves in the room. "One outlet was just a pipe sticking out of the wall, with blue flame coming out of it, but I managed to turn it off," he stated. "How to turn them all off was confusing, but I did it."

• • • • • •

Massive cavern under New York City
Negotiations bring underground neighborhood to light

NEW YORK CITY — A massive underground cavern was revealed late today under the metropolis. Broad entrances to the cavern are present in four of the city's boroughs, and structures that include dwellings, libraries, and police stations have been constructed underground. "You could be walking along a street at night and not even realize you had walked into the cavern," one witness explained.

Initially the cavern was to be kept secret, but negotiations with residents led to a compromise in which only nearby residents would be informed of its existence; further discussion led to this evening's revelation and vows of complete transparency.

South pole mission participants still need some convincing
Laxatives involved in mission training program

LOS ANGELES — Reports tonight indicated that a local man is still attempting to convince friends from his high school and university days, as well as his brother, to go on a planned mission to the south pole. "My brother wants to pull out because our family is breaking up," the man explained, "and despite my trying to convince them all, they're still not sure."

The group reportedly took city buses to the training hospital for the first step, which involved taking a laxative.

· · · · · ·

Airport staff "crazy"
Mini shovels have razor-sharp blades

NEW YORK CITY — Disembarking from an airliner in the city, a Los Angeles man reported tonight that the airport clerk "was a little crazy." The clerk was allegedly in possession of instruments described as "these little mini shovels with razor-sharp blades."

The two men had a heated verbal dispute, characterized by what the witness described as the clerk's "attitude." Subsequently, the clerk followed the man through the airport, and on catching up with him, allegedly apologized for his behavior.

Midwest nuclear plot

OMAHA, NEB. — A visitor to the area allegedly learned of a plot for the city to be "secretly nuked." Most residents were reportedly unable to evacuate the city, but the man and a friend were able to fly out at the last minute, allegedly with the assistance of "some generals" at the airport.

· · · · · ·

Renowned alien investigator in diner incident
Restaurant destroyed in explosion

LOS ANGELES — A renowned alien investigator was seen at the airport recently, dining at an eatery with a local resident. The resident reports that an alien, "disguised as a hippie" and sitting across the counter from them, used its extremely long fingers to try to steal something from the investigator. The pair threw bread and other items they found at hand at the alien, but the creature allegedly managed to

enlist the assistance of a robot that rapidly hurled cutlery back at them, rendering the bread projectiles ineffective. The robot then displayed large red numbers that rapidly counted down. The pair reportedly then ran out the door just as the eatery exploded.

· · · · · ·

Renovations induce sadness

LOCAL — A man reported feelings of sadness tonight as he helped his father prepare to rebuild part of the basement. "We were moving stuff into bins," the man explained.

· · · · · ·

Bus trip passes unusual balconies

New invention widens armrests

WESTERN CANADA — A visitor to the region reported today that he was on a cross-country bus trip, "crossing the prairies with five cool people." The traveling companions were allegedly "all new to me" and talked about "their intense lives." One of the passengers was reportedly wearing "weird blue-face makeup."

Initially the man claimed to be with the group in a new shopping mall under the north side of Wellington Street in Ottawa. The man described wandering along the mall, from the Château Laurier hotel toward the East Block of Parliament, "looking for a decent coffee." Although he managed to identify a place to get coffee up ahead, he claimed to have gotten distracted with his new friends. One of the group, described as "a Jewish girl," explained that "old icons are replaced by new ones."

On the bus, the man alleges that he "hung out the window" and saw a friend on his balcony, "one of several oddly tiered irregular balconies on the west side of the building." His friend's was reportedly "just below and on the left." The balconies were further described as "of various sizes, but all of them were wide and stretched out, not too sharply down, like the rice field terraces in Indonesia."

The man's friend reportedly showed him several of his inventions, including a device to make the armrest of chairs wider for men. "Not upholstered chairs," the witness explained, "but office or lawn chair–type chairs."

The bus's progress was eventually halted by a gas leak.

• • • • • •

Foot severed
Patient hesitates to trouble doctor

CITY — An area resident reports tonight that his right foot had somehow been severed at the ankle. The bone was described as "a narrow black rod" that had "oily black gunk" surrounding it. The man allegedly requested a doctor to help reattach it, although at first he claims he hesitated to bother her. "I knew it had to be done, as it was starting to rot," he explained, "and I knew if it took too long it was not going to be viable."

• • • • • •

Maritime voyage marred by broken glass
New colors described

WESTERN EUROPE — A man reported tonight that the German train he was a passenger on became a ship and undertook a lengthy voyage. There were many other passengers aboard "to chat with," the man claimed, and allegedly "there was broken glass, but we swept it up."

The man reported chatting with three older women: one was named Hurley, another Maxwell, and the third whose name "I forgot." Allegedly there were also some young people aboard. Two colors came up in the discussions, named Selenicas and Cedar Blond. At press time a more detailed description of these colors was unavailable.

· · · · · ·

Time-travel incidents around park

Actor in public sex act

CITY — Describing his fellow residents as "unique and cool," an area man reported tonight that they were all living by a big park. A Neanderthal was allegedly "sent back to our time" and was living among them. While he was in the park, the witness explained that he knew the Neanderthal was "there somewhere too."

Across the street a woman was reportedly getting settled in her new home. Described as overweight, the woman reportedly had eyes that were fully irises, with no white, "like a deer."

The man claimed he was able to visit the 1960s by "clicking" on the image, "the way you do on a web page." Just before he made

the click, the man reports that he saw a well-known cinematic actor standing against the side of the brick stoop of a building in the park—"Maybe it was a school"—and allowing himself to be stripped for a blow job. "It wasn't me doing it," the man claimed, "but I was right there. It was like I was doing it but not doing it, watching but doing it."

The actor was allegedly dressed like an Italian laborer from the 1930s, in a white tank-top undershirt, suspenders, and gray flannel pants. Described as "much thinner and slighter than the real actor," the man had a dark complexion and wore a mask that had an orange carrot-shaped nose and "a white part that covered around his eyes, although it had eye holes." The actor was reportedly grinning, enjoying the stripping and the blow job.

⸱ ⸱ ⸱ ⸱ ⸱ ⸱

Man killed in political massacre

Claims machine-gun fire "painless," vacates body

LOCAL — An area man reported tonight that he became involved with a political group allegedly tasked with "dealing with" a group of racists described as "very dangerous." The man and his cohorts managed to lure the racist faction to gather at a specific house, "and once we had them inside, we had to kill them." The man claimed that this was "a good thing, not a bad thing, because they were doing so much damage in other ways." Details of the racists' identities were not immediately apparent.

The man reported that he was in the front room of the house and was sent into the back room. "My people had the guns," the man explained, "and I was afraid that the people in my group wouldn't know who I was. I was afraid of getting shot." The atmosphere in the house was described as "tense," and the man claims that when someone started shouting, he was forced to pull out a machine gun and shoot those in the room. One of the racists, described as standing "in the middle, to the left," allegedly pulled out his own machine gun, and pointed it directly at the witness, and fired. The weapon "sparked or flashed blue," and the man reports that he didn't feel any pain, but he knew he was dead.

"I left my body," the man reported, "and I

looked back to see it, but even though I knew it was me slumped there on the floor, I couldn't see it." The man did witness one of his group enter the room, described as "the Buddha, or at least at a powerful Buddhist spirit." The man allegedly patted him on the back, "but I don't think he noticed me." The man claims that the associate was there "doing something good."

The man subsequently returned to the front room and said good-bye to a former student, described as "in her black underwear." The woman apparently understood that the witness had left his body, and she was described as "sad, crying," but gave the man a hug. Others present were reportedly unable to see that the man had left his body.

• • • • • •

New inconvenient driveway process

Houses in "conformist" suburb painted vivid colors

SAN FRANCISCO BAY AREA — A man reported moving to a "rustic yet conformist tract housing suburb" of the city with "lots of trees." The houses in the neighborhood were described as "dusty, not bright, pastel greens and yellows and blues." The man allegedly moved into one of the blue houses that included a strip of siding. The exact color of the house is described by the hex color code #00A294, and the yellow houses were described as #C2B515.

The man claimed that he "met everyone," and talked to all the neighbors, and "made out with a chubby guy from next door." The new resident stated that "I wanted to get to know him better." Described as older than the witness, the neighbor allegedly told him that he was "old enough to know what I want now."

While driving into the driveway of his new house, the man stated that there was a fence he had to drive over, with a strip of aluminum that matched the house's siding. The man reported that he "had to take the strip of stuff off the wire fence, then drive over it." A passenger in the vehicle explained that it was necessary to do this each time, a process that the witness described as "inconvenient."

· · · · · ·

New dance craze tires participants

"The rage" a type of twist

CITY — A local man reported participating in a new dance craze called "the rage." Described as "like the twist," the man alleged that "Everyone was sick of it," and he thus proceeded to take the needle off the record "to help the DJ." Witness reports indicate that it made a loud scratchy sound, and the man reported that "I dropped the tone arm

again," resulting in a staticky scratch.

· · · · · ·

Wedding invite dilemma

Roommate's embalming hobby leads to murder

LOCAL — Tasked with sending out invites to a wedding, a local man reported that he wasn't sure whether to send out invitations in gold foil–lined envelopes—disliked by his roommate—or to send out a video movie. The film contained a murder, the man alleged, and thus did not seem appropriate for a wedding invitation.

Another roommate, known as Dad but not the actual father of the man or his other roommate, allegedly became interested in embalming and burial. The man was described as going farther afield over time to obtain bodies. Eventually the man reportedly suspected that the roommate had committed murder to obtain bodies, alleging that "there was guts in the rear window of his car."

. . . .

Astral travel to Elvis's room

LOCAL — An area man made what he described as an "out-of-control" visit to a room where pop musician Elvis Presley was. The man allegedly "zapped around from one part of this room to another, just flitting like a spark." With allegedly no control over his movement, the man stated that in each new position, high or low in the room, he found himself in a different orientation, often upside-down or sideways.

. . . .

Overseas work-trip departure incurs delays

Supermarket bureaucracy cited

TOKAI REGION, JAPAN — Employed as entertainers in a bar for Japanese gangsters, a local man reports that he and his roommate performed "corny little skits for the bar patrons." Even though the pair experienced no violence or threats, the man said he felt that "We couldn't say no to the work."

The gangsters then allegedly asked the pair to do an out-of-town job in Toronto. When they arrived at the train station where their employers had arranged to pick them up, the man allegedly realized he had forgotten the props for some of the skits and had to run back home. Once he'd returned to the station, he was forced to make a second excursion, reportedly to a supermarket to buy "some stuff for the trip," including orange juice and a medium-size pumpkin.

The checkout system at the supermarket was described as "incredibly bureaucratic": Customers were obliged to take a little number tag, then go through a metal detector, then give the tag to the correct cashier. The man reportedly ignored the staffer who tried to give him the number tag, and barged through the metal detector. "I felt I didn't have time for this," the man said, and allegedly then paid and hurried out.

The man's roommate and the gangster boss were waiting in his car, described as "a typical Japanese gangster station wagon." They were reportedly annoyed at being kept waiting, as the supermarket excursion had taken "quite a while." The roommate then said, "I've got a message from two of your good old friends," explaining that she had met them at the station while waiting for the car. "Who were they?" the man reportedly asked, but the roommate claimed not to know, stating that "They said you'd know" and that the message from his friends was "Don't get your can kicked."

Huge party, plastic participants

CITY — An area resident reported tonight that he attended a "huge, wild" party that was held in front of a big house. Among the partygoers, the man alleged, were many "plastic" people.

Travelers board separate planes

Flight attendants mystified at mix-up

LAX — A Los Angeles couple headed out on the same trip boarded separate planes tonight, sources indicate. "There was a last-minute change of aircraft, and my friend didn't hear the announcement," one of the men claimed,

"and we spoke to different flight attendants."

As the planes taxied away from the terminal, the two men could see each other from the windows of the aircraft. "I saw him sitting there, so I got the plane to stop so he could get on ours," the man explained. The second man was reportedly red-faced when he boarded the correct aircraft. At press time flight attendants were still trying to ascertain the cause of the error.

Man instructs scientists on acid use

LOCAL — An area man reported advising a group of scientists on the proper use of acids in the production of medications. "The third acid should definitely be used," the man recalled explaining to them.

Man time-travels, avoids self

Hotel described as "dingy"

LOCAL — An area resident reported today that he traveled back in time, but "I knew that I had to avoid meeting my old self." The man described staying at the same hotel, described as "dingy" and constructed in a "shoddy and cheap" manner, where the older version of himself was staying. "I almost met myself once," the man alleged, and admits that "I thought of spying on myself. What would I look like? How would I feel?"

· · · · · ·

Atomic plant searched for aliens

UNDISCLOSED LOCATION — A man described "sneaking around" an atomic plant tonight, and allegedly engaged in several secret meetings. "Our goal was to try to gather evidence of an alien connection," the man explained. Other members of the search

party were described as young men.

Diapers in cocktail bar

LOCAL — Reports indicate that a man asked, "Why would you bring diapers to a cocktail bar?" The circumstances and situation that led to this query remain vague tonight. No further information was immediately available. This story will be updated as developments warrant.

· · · · · ·

Concert tickets cost more than double

Group priced out of attendance

THE OLD HOMETOWN — On a winter night recently when snow had accumulated on the ground, a man reported that a concert to be held in the man's one-time primary school was heavily advertised in local media. Along with his father, a former colleague from work, and several others, the man went to the school auditorium.

When the group arrived they discovered that tickets for the concert were $75, not $35 as they had allegedly been told. After some discussion of the options—to return later to ask for a discount was proposed—the group decided that they could not attend the concert, and attending a film screening was reportedly discussed as an alternative.

One of the organizers of the event turned out to be another of the man's former colleagues. Described as "all over, for a lot of reasons," the man was alleged to "have his fingers in a lot of different pies."

· · · · · ·

Late-night visit leads to computer troubleshooting

Secret back stairs lead half a flight down

CITY — Tonight the wife of a local man, whom the witness described as "an occasional hookup," allegedly knocked on the witness's apartment door and requested to be allowed in so that the man could help her with a computer issue. "I was almost certain she would pick the lock or had a secret key, so I quietly slipped on the chain while talking to her through the door," the man explained. The woman, described as "really insistent," was eventually dissuaded and went away.

The man returned to his living room, but alleges that he then heard someone in the bathroom. He discovered a grade-school acquaintance had entered the bathroom via a secret set of back stairs that connected the bathroom to what the interloper described as "my room," in a dark storeroom half a flight down. The visitor reportedly brought a woman with him, and they were "hanging out" in the witness's bathroom. The homeowner told them that he couldn't believe they had essentially broken into his apartment, but the pair offered no response. The man informed them that if they were going to hang out, they also had to admit the woman who had visited earlier.

The woman was quickly located in the hall outside the apartment, and when she entered, the resident stated that "I tried to help with her computer." The device's operating system was described as "weird," however; "The menus wouldn't appear unless you put the mouse over the word, and they were written downward and to the right on a zigzag. The whole look and feel was this vampire Gothic thing." The software at issue was stated to be modem software, but the man reported that "I couldn't figure out where to download or upload the files she wanted." The woman subsequently talked him through it, but the resident couldn't control the mouse. "It was very frustrating—the screen would zip out of sight at the slightest touch, or it would rotate and wobble, sometimes turning itself inside out when I moved the mouse." Finally the man allegedly told her that she must have the mouse sensitivity set too high.

· · · · · ·

Elf images alive

Earth energy cited

LOCAL — Elf images are alive, a local man reported tonight. Allegedly related to the phenomenon is a power that is buried in the earth, described as "the cause of earthquakes." The man claimed that his car "runs differently" when parked over the spot, but admitted that "No one believes me."

Delays at hotel check-in

Father-actor requests phone book; paper clips scattered

EASTERN CANADA — A visitor reportedly took his infant nephew on a holiday to the region. At the check-in desk of their accommodations, described as "a big chain hotel," the man allegedly tried to phone home, but "it wouldn't work." He described speaking with various operators and spending "a long time" on hold.

The check-in process was reportedly delayed by other hotel guests, described as "middle-aged and older" women. The man compared children with the other guests, and expressed shock that his nephew was so small. After completing check-in, the man described entering the restaurant behind the check-in desk. The man's traveling companion was "suddenly my dad, but he was an adventure-film actor." Described as "tired and hungry," the man's father was sitting at a corner table with another man, wearing a suit; the pair of them were reportedly eating.

The older man reportedly then asked the witness for three things: a government phone book, more food (the witness suggested he have a burger, and politely asked the other man what he wanted to order), and a phone. The witness returned to the reception, privately hoping that no one on staff was upset with him for writing out a complaint about not being able to use his phone card earlier. At the desk he asked for the government phone book. The clerk on the counter explained that the government phone book was simply the blue pages in the regular phone book. The man asked her where to order food, even though "I already knew," to which the clerk responded, "The cashier, of course."

The man stated that later, he saw his father was still eating, and a peer group from his middle school days were lounging in the hotel lobby. The witness described "talking and joking" with the group. At one point he allegedly dropped a box of paper clips, which didn't spill, and said to one of his middle school peers, "If you were really mean, you would have kicked these all over the *genkan*." [*Editor's note:* A *genkan* (玄関) is the traditional entry area in Japanese houses and apartments, similar to a Western porch or mud room, where outdoor shoes are kept.] The hotel's *genkan* was reportedly half a flight of stairs down from the lobby and had "a huge door." The man described it as "a hilarious image," the paper clips scattering uniformly over every corner of the stairs.

Walking down the hallway to the right of the *genkan,* the man explained that he was headed to the cafeteria. The building felt more like an institution than a hotel, with an air of "a 1950s schoolhouse." Two women from his middle school days accompanied him, and one of them humorously suggested, "You could be put in detention." The witness then reportedly joke that "They would force me to marry someone from the women's detention center."

Rocky social interactions

"They ditched me"

ON CAMPUS — A former student of the university reported tonight that he was on campus with some "new friends"—two women and a man. The quartet went to a movie hall that had a green color scheme and high ceilings, and later moved to a similar hall with a black theme. Describing the interactions with the others, the man stated that "We weren't clicking. Something was off."

At one point the man had to ask, "Say that again?" because he couldn't grasp what the others were saying. Explaining his confusion, he told them that "I've been away from English-speaking people for a long time." None of the trio asked him to elaborate, "as would have been friendly," the man explained, but instead simply replied with "Oh." At that point the man alleges that the trio "ditched me."

Later, the four were reunited in the black-themed movie hall when the man reportedly returned there to look for something he had misplaced as well as his bag, "which I'd forgotten there." The man also reported that he walked through the pedestrian tunnels that link the various campus buildings, finding them "more elaborate than in my day. It was like the first time I'd seen them."

Peaceful airport takeover

Passengers assured of tampon stockpiles

MALTA — Passengers waiting for a flight to continental Europe Monday were shocked when terrorists appeared to take over the airport. Several passengers in the departure lounge waiting to board the 737 stated they were suspicious at seeing personnel in nonstandard uniforms hurrying through the airport before the takeover. "They didn't want to blow anything up or kill anyone," explained the witness. "They just wanted to take over."

A long and unextraordinary boarding announcement on the PA system, "Now boarding, Flight 852, Gate 16," was reportedly suddenly interrupted by the sound of a scuffle, followed by the voice of a different woman. Passengers report the voice on the PA now was "much deeper" and "had a Greek accent." The terrorists allegedly read a statement on the PA:

> Passengers departing on flight 852, have no fears about traveling to Europe. There are plenty of tampons on board the aircraft. There are also no shortages of tampons anywhere in the EC. All cities have large stockpiles of feminine hygiene products.

Doctor's bag revealed, painted

LOCAL — Reports tonight indicate that a local man's maternal grandmother showed him a doctor's bag that had belonged to her ex-lover of many years ago. The lover had allegedly been a failed medical student. The grandmother then proceeded to paint the bag green. The man and his brother-in-law gave the woman what he described as "big hugs."

British music kept behind the counter

LOCAL — Shopping in a city record store, a man alleged that the British section was kept behind the counter. Perusing the CDs in that section, the man allegedly found an album by a band called Cunning Dolls. The album art was reportedly a series of small dolls depicted "playing bad tricks." The cov-er art of another album in the section depicted a man wearing gray and photographed in black-and-white. Shelved next to each other were two albums by a folk singer named Peggy Pregnant and another singer named Priggy Pregnant, both of which the man described as "controversial."

. . . .

Nuclear waste dump slated for South LA

Tomatoes ignored

LOS ANGELES — A Black teenager working in a very busy back office at LAX described his experience of racism tonight. An older Black man made a detailed speech in the office on topic of political corruption, outlining how the Watts neighborhood had been ignored and would now be the site of a nuclear waste dump. The man was described as "very disgruntled."

The older man had tomatoes that he wanted to share, described as "beautiful," but an older woman expressed concern about how the tomatoes were served, allegedly insisting on no salt and no spices, as they might contain caffeine. A little girl standing at the window noticed an erstwhile acquaintance from New Zealand in the building across the alley, reportedly "talking on a cell phone." The others remembered her, and went to the window to look, in the process ignoring the tomatoes.

. . . .

Job hunt mistaken for "some sex thing"

CITY — Reports indicate that a local man spent the night at an all-night computer place in order to "hunt for a job." When he went to the restroom, he allegedly found it to be "very dirty," and claimed that "I couldn't whiz" because the manager-caretaker stood waiting for him outside the toilet stall. The staffer allegedly told him, in a friendly way, "Go home and have relations with safe people." The man explained that the manager assumed he was doing "some sex thing" on the company's computers. In the stall, the man reportedly found a wallet and a day planner, and passed them out to the staff member.

. . . .

Snooze until crunchy gray

CITY — A local man reported this morning that he hit the snooze button on his alarm, planning to awaken again and "meet myself back here." The snooze button was set not for a specific time but for a color, described as "a dark-red, speckly, crunchy gray."

. . . .

Shoes stolen on Hollywood Boulevard

Footwear "a really nice shade of light lemon yellow"

HOLLYWOOD, CALIF. — A neighborhood office worker reports that his tennis shoes were stolen on Hollywood Boulevard. "I was coming up out of the subway at Hollywood and Highland and saw them sitting there on the curb where I'd left them," the man told journalists. While he was approaching the curb to retrieve his shoes, he noticed passers-by looking at the shoes in curiosity. "They were a really nice shade of light

lemon yellow," the alleged victim claimed. When he was within thirty feet of the shoes, "a couple of big-boned women" picked up the shoes and walked off with them. Catching up with them, he reportedly confronted the women, who would not return the shoes, as "they didn't believe they were mine." Investigations are ongoing. This story will be updated as events warrant.

• • • • • •

Homophobic slur cast at rail reunion

Check-in process "interminable"

WESTERN CANADA — A visitor to the region reported attending a workplace reunion that was held on a moving train, headed east to west across the prairie provinces. The check-in process for the reunion allegedly "took hours," and rather than endure the long wait, the man claimed that he simply avoided the line-ups. One of the staffers on the registration line reportedly knew the man, and when she announced that she was going to read aloud some of his writing, he left.

The man stated that he sat at a group table for dinner, where one of the other reunion attendees allegedly asked in a loud voice, "Is that that faggot?" The verbal aggressor was described as balding and wearing black sunglasses. The witness reported that "I wasn't offended, but I also wasn't into communicating on that level." Removing himself from the table, the man reportedly then ate dinner alone.

• • • • • •

Middle school acquaintance in prison frame-up

Aliens on-site doing "weird psychology"

PARIS — Admitting that he was "emotionally involved" with the prisoner, a visitor to the city reported that a middle school acquaintance was in prison. The man himself was also temporarily imprisoned for committing perjury during the trial but was subsequently released. The acquaintance asked that the man "stay in with him," as he was allegedly framed to wind up there. The man reported that within the prison, gray aliens were conducting experiments and doing "weird psychology." The man stated that "The road we all traveled goes right past the prison gates."

Later on, the story was reported on television, on a program called *Communion*. "It was on television," the man explained, "but it wasn't fiction. I'm there acting in the show every week." The television series moved through the back streets of Paris, from northwest to southeast, covering a new street each week. The man stated that "I think I'll be forty by the time we get to the Bastille."

· · · · · ·

City "redone"

Fire, burglary in castle accommodations

OTTAWA, CANADA —Visiting the city for the first time in many years, a former resident reported tonight that the city "has been totally redone." Staying in a castle as his accommodations, the man claimed that a German visitor to the city broke into his room "to get paint." Later there was a fire in the castle while the man was doing some contract typing, and he reconfirmed his flight out.

· · · · · ·

Streets dark, shops blacked out

Motorcyclist hookup doesn't stop

CITY — An area resident described hearing a motorcycle driving down his street tonight. When it stopped, the man allegedly thought it might be a man he occasionally hooks up with. The witness stated that he was on the street "with all the movie the-

aters" and that the motorcyclist turned left, "away from me," without noticing the man or stopping.

Turning the next corner onto a wider boulevard, the man stated that "it was really dark," and when he came up to the convenience store, he was fearful as the store and all the others were completely dark. The man reported that he saw a note taped to the door of the convenience store, but "I didn't go that far," instead returning to the street with the cinemas. The man stated that "I wasn't sure if it was a power failure or what." This story will be updated as new details emerge.

Sibling requests assistance for Mont Blanc trip

Mountain "a weird 1950s resort"

FRENCH-ITALIAN BORDER— A local man reported tonight that his older brother requested his assistance in planning a trip for his children to the top of Mont Blanc. "He phoned me to come and help him," the man alleged. "It was like a spy phone call." The man's brother reportedly called and said, "Come to level 6 on the mountain," then hung up, "even though I knew it was him and he knew that I knew."

Several children joined in the excursion, and the man reported that "I realized too late that I had done all the prep work for the same trip last year" and that he would needlessly have to repeat it all. Mont Blanc was described as extremely high and volcanic, with "beautiful" hot springs that were said to resemble the hotel pools on Santorini in Greece. The lava flows were allegedly "a mile high," and the mountain had many visitors, including some purported gangsters who appeared to be ancient Greeks.

Despite the fact that the excursion took place in the summer season, the mountain was laid out like a ski run, with no trees. The man described the area as "like a weird 1950s resort place" and compared the atmosphere to the wilderness around Mount Rushmore in South Dakota.

Film costar "vivid" but "disinterested"

"Perspective" gained

LOS ANGELES — A local man reported appearing in a movie wearing a gray beret and sporting a beard. The other actor in the film was a man who played a bartender. The witness alleges that "We were trying to accomplish something significant despite the fact we all knew it was an act." The bartender, described as "vividly himself," reportedly acted "distant" but not indignant about being there. "It was more like he was disinterested,"

the man explained, "and just putting in an appearance. It was good for me, as it gives me a sense of perspective."

· · · · · ·

New alcoholism drug

CITY — Reports tonight indicate that a new drug has been released. The medication allegedly causes hallucinations in order to fight alcoholism. The generic name of the drug was reported as either "esqureida" or "esquerida."

· · · · · ·

Party for mother, grandparents

Several deceased attend

THE OLD HOMETOWN — Reports tonight indicate that a man returned to the region in order to attend a birthday party for his mother, deceased more than a decade ago. Other party guests allegedly included the man's similarly dead grandparents. The man stated that "they were all happy to see me."

Shoes unable to ascend sloping floor

DOWNTOWN — A local man reportedly attended a film screening tonight at a movie theater, but was unable to walk up the slope of the raked floor because "my shoes were too slick-soled." The man allegedly then ascended the incline "on my butt, backwards," while holding onto the legs of theater seats for leverage. "Everyone was laughing at a trailer on the screen," the man claimed.

• • • • • •

Desert bus trip to concert

Event held in tent

NEGEV DESERT, ISRAEL — A visitor to the holy land reported today that his father had given him tickets to a concert. The man allegedly traveled to the concert venue by bus, through the desert, and explained that aboard the bus, he befriended "a straight couple." The concert was held in a tent, and audience members sat on benches.

Park visit to study faces

Visitor assists elderly man on walk

OTTAWA, CANADA — A visitor to the area reported flying to the region today on a small jet that stopped at various places in Eastern Siberia, eventually crossing the Bering Strait. The man stated that he flew over the city and walked around a large park in order to "look at the faces, and see the depth of the personality in each one." Other park visitors included "an opera diva" along with many detailed faces with European features. The man admitted that he knew he should call an old friend who lived in the city but that "I was enjoying the park."

Near an outdoor book sale, the visitor allegedly encountered an "old man" who was browsing the books. The man reportedly asked the visitor to support his arm not by using words but "just by touching my arm." The man was described as wearing dark glasses, "but he wasn't blind." The visitor explained that he supported the man's arm "for a while." The man led the visitor up a hill out of town. The visitor stated that "I didn't know where we were going." Another man, standing near a shop "over to my left" was observed watching them. When he met his gaze, the visitor claimed that he raised his eyebrows to say, "I don't know what's going on either." The old man then walked over a couple of gentle hills to where his people were waiting for him. When he got near the group, he reportedly let go of the visitor's arm and waved good-bye.

Canadian park overrun with venomous snakes

Visitor bitten on sofa

CENTRAL MANITOBA, CANADA — Today a visitor to the region reported visiting a park with several rivers that allegedly feed into the Mississippi River. The visitor stated that the park was home to many "huge" venomous snakes, and several people were reportedly employed full-

time to kill them. The man reported that while he was sitting on a sofa, "someone agitated them" and three of the snakes bit him.

Date request declined at baths

"Maybe if I were Israeli"

CITY — Tonight a local man reported visiting a "huge, cavernous" public baths. Women were among the bathers, including the man's erstwhile employer, but the clientele was described as "mostly men walking around." The man stated that there was "this one guy that I liked," described as "a pretty blond," and the man allegedly asked him "to go out with me some time." The blond turned down the invitation, and the witness explained that "I knew it was because I'm not pretty enough. He's out of my league."

The blond reportedly then stated matter-of-factly that he would date the witness "if I were Israeli or something and he could learn the language." The man reported seeing the blond around the baths several more times, and stated that the man was part of a group, "an actors' group, I think." Their passing interactions were described as "friendly," but the man admits that "there's this awareness that I am interested and he's not."

• • • • • •

Man disembarks train

SAN DIEGO — A man reportedly disembarked the train today in the Finest City in possession of three objects: a watch strap, a spoon, and a fork.

French café refuses service

Cook "surly"

RURAL FRANCE — Sources tonight report that a man and his childhood friend acted as tour guides in the French countryside for a small group of Japanese visitors and a renowned American film director. Activities reportedly included attending film screenings and riding bicycles.

When the group entered a small country café, the

woman who ran the establishment, described as "surly," refused to cook for them, forcing the group to wait. The man alleges that "we brought some of our own food, and ate it in the café, and then we wouldn't back down." The witness described the film director as "bored and hungry."

• • • • • •

Emotional reunion

LOS ANGELES — Reports tonight indicate that a man was reunited with his roommate after a lengthy absence. The woman reportedly hugged the man and cried. When asked what was bothering her and making her so upset, the woman allegedly explained that "It's the details. All the little details."

Revolting beverages served

Squid ink, potato juice among offerings

AT THE MALL — A local man reported tonight that he and a friend were at the mall. The pair decided to get refreshments at the Orange Julius stand, and subsequently chatted with the attendant at the nearby motivational speaker booth "as a way to harass him."

The man's companion allegedly "just said yes" to whatever the woman running the Orange Julius stand offered him, mostly because she was speaking Japanese and his language skills were weak. The pair ended up with an all-you-can-drink "gross drink plan" that cost ¥3,379 (about $26) each. The first beverage served was orange juice mixed with Coca-Cola in a large pitcher, described as "one and a half or two quarts," with the cola separated out on the bottom, which the witness described as "okay, but gross." Then next beverage was squid ink and potato juice in the same size pitcher, with the squid ink on top. The witness stated that the men found the drink unappetizing, "so we just paid and left."

The pair reportedly then visited the speakers' lounge, but no speech was being given. Instead "there was just a video playing," with several spectators, including "an obese woman," in the lounge watching the video and reportedly "looking motivated."

Car-train collision narrowly avoided

Tracks mistaken for road

TOKAI REGION, JAPAN — An area resident reported driving his friend's car in order for the pair to take a test in another town. The man allegedly mistook the Tōkaidō Main Line tracks for a road and turned onto the rail bed. He then attempted to back up, but there was a train rapidly approaching. The rail-crossing gates lowered across the road, narrowly missing the car, and the train stopped before striking the vehicle. The man reportedly drove away, avoiding the gaze of the railroad staff, and reported that he subsequently "let her drive."

Scottish film screening

Moviegoer avoids stepping on fingers

LOCAL — An area resident reported tonight that he watched a Scottish comedy film at a local movie house, sitting "right up front, right under the screen." The film's plot allegedly involved a woman who worked as a hotel staffer, a male bellhop, and a maid who snuck into a guest room and plotted to steal something.

The man reported that he snuck out of the theater near the end of the first act, returning home to "pig out on junk food." There were reportedly so many people reclining in the aisle of the theater that he had to be very careful not to step on anyone's fingers in the darkened hall. The other audience members' fingers were described as looking "like spiders scuttling out of my way as they moved."

· · · · · ·

Apartment looks different "psychically"

Globe pushed through table

CITY — Reports today indicate that a local resident found his apartment was different than it looked before. "There was a globe there," the man explained, "and I put my hands on it and pushed it down through the table." The witness alleges that "At first I thought I'd been robbed" but then realized that the apartment's appearance dif-

fered psychically: "Things look different than they do non-psychically."

Aggression at gay-straight encounter night

Toilets "overflowing"

CITY — "Volcanoes of shit" were reportedly oozing out of the floor in several places tonight in a local bar. An area resident stated that the excretions were in a variety of colors. In his attempt to find a toilet stall, the man claimed that the stalls were all "either occupied or overflowing with shit."

The man reportedly sat at a table where two men and two women were seated, explaining that "I thought they were gay because it was a gay bar."

One of the men allegedly said, "So you're one of the freaks," in a manner that was described as "quite aggressive and with no respect, but not threat-ening." The witness then found out the bar was hosting a "gay-straight en-counter night," and quick-ly left the table.

. . . . . .

Former boss in Room 15

Witness pressured to complete tasks

LOCAL — Reports today indicate that a local man's antagonistic former boss was in Room 15, and later Room 14, of his erstwhile high school. The woman allegedly stated that "Your homework isn't finished. The big guy needs it by 5." The man claims that he paused, and considered saying "Fuck you," but instead said "It'll be ready," reportedly "just like I al-ways did."

. . . . . .

Large supermarket devoid of appealing food

"Trick" escalators add to confusion

CITY — On an excursion today to visit an acquain-tance who lives some dis-tance out in the coun-tryside, a local resident reported that his family waited in the car for him to buy snacks. The man explained that he wan-dered alone in the large supermarket, alleging that "there's no food that I want."

The supermarket was described as on two floors with "trick" escalators— the moving stairs trans-ported shoppers to unex-pected parts of the store. The man ran into a work colleague, and the pair re-portedly discussed the es-calators, with his colleague agreeing that "they're tricky." Unlike the witness, his colleague stated that she was able to find food.

The man explained that "I felt really rushed, run-ning all around this store that has nothing to buy," knowing that people were waiting for him. Final-ly the man purchased an egg-salad sandwich.

· · · · · ·

Men seen on golf course

"Happy" to caddy for friends

SUBURBIA — A local man reports that he and his husband were on a golf course today. The witness stated that he was "happy" to act as caddy for some friends who were playing golf, as the quartet could "get some exercise and chat."

Apocalypse begins

Aliens explain destruction process

WESTERN CANADA — Human technological activity has led to the imminent destruction of the moon, it was revealed today. This in turn will lead to the destruction of the Earth. A former area resident accompanied his twin brothers into the countryside for a last look at the planet before its demise, the man explained. "People were calm, but they had given up on their daily routines," he said. He also alleged that a flock of sheep had been left to wander through a field of dye plants owned by a local woman. Many of the sheep had become dyed gray, but some were also dyed in unusual shades of yellow and blue. A well-known actor was allegedly seen wandering the hills foraging for food with her husband. The man spoke to her and explained that they had met several weeks ago, but the actor only remembered one of the man's brothers. Her husband, the man alleged, "was completely drunk." The group proceeded down into a metal structure that led into "a valley, or a shelter, or something similarly huge," but the structure was open to the sky and afforded little protection from the impending apocalypse.

In one of the rooms in

the structure a meeting was allegedly being held with visiting aliens. They were not present to offer help, but to explain the mechanics of the destruction of the moon and Earth. The man didn't attend the meeting but sat on the floor outside the room with a sheaf of papers, planning to "read or write something." The twins elected to attend the meeting, but to do so allegedly had to change their physical form. While one twin kept his clothes, the other went naked and assumed the form of a child, "almost like an alien too." The clothed twin became "muscled and oiled, like a Roman slave." When the three aliens came out of the room, they appeared as older women. The naked twin requested that the man write down the name and phone number of one of the women, as she had kept some of his mail. She was a neighbor of the men, although they had not met before. The witness explained that he wrote the information down with paintbrushes, which made the information hard to read "but very colorful." He subsequently rewrote it.

The group moved to a cabin on a wide flat plain, and described the weather as "weird," most likely due to the impending disaster. Large chunks of watery slush allegedly fell from the sky, causing earthquakes. During one earthquake the men braced themselves inside the cabin, fearful that the slush would strike the building. "It was bright out," the man explained, "but it was raining heavily." The colors of the landscape were also allegedly very unnatural, with the ground appearing bright red.

House party "kind of Euro"
Host denies drug allegations

LOS ANGELES — Reports tonight indicate that a man attended a house party with his husband. The host was allegedly a man described as "a performer" and "kind of Euro." The witness reported that "everyone thinks he's a drug dealer." The host denied the allegation, to which several of the guests replied, "That's what they all say."

Turtle hides on wall

"Beautiful" partridge made of light

IN THE MOUNTAINS — A visitor to the area reported walking through a dark cave, where he allegedly spotted a turtle hiding above eye level on the left wall. The man stated that he encouraged the turtle "to come down and show itself." When the reptile complied, it was a partridge-shaped bird, described as "beautiful" and made of light, with supersaturated strands of color forming its outlines. The witness stated that where its eyes and brain would be, however, was "just empty space."

Copies replacing originals

Violent solution explored

CITY — A local man reported tonight that "copies are taking the place of real people." No specific evidence for the allegation was provided, but the man stated that "I have to sneak up on them and slit their throats."

· · · · · ·

Drug-sniffing squirrel scores big

Massive cache of marijuana uncovered

LOS ANGELES — A local man reported today that he and his husband were in possession of a drug-sniffing squirrel. "It was a tiny little thing," the man alleged, and they set the creature outside near the place they were tasked with guarding. The site was described as "like a shop" but "with no one else around."

The rodent subsequently sat down on the concrete floor, indicating that there were drugs nearby. The man and his husband stated that they walked upwind of where the squirrel had sat down, and on lifting up grate in the floor, discovered several massive bundles of marijuana.

"I realized it was so valuable that someone dangerous might be coming back for it," the man explained, and for that reason allegedly sought out a gun. The weapon was described as "a weird electronic contraption" that was blue in color with an LED readout. The revolver barrel reportedly had six differently sized and shaped bullets in it.

When the duo sat down on the ground in the front of the shop, the man admits that "I accidentally fired a bullet," which whizzed back and forth over their heads for a few seconds. Although the inadvertent discharge hadn't been loud, the electronics in the gun alerted the alarm company that it had been fired, and an alarm went off. Crowds of

people reportedly started gathering in the street in front of the shop, and the alarm company's patrol car "raced up." The man stated that he fully expected the police to arrive and that he would be arrested.

· · · · · ·

Gay camp awards car

Hard work studying, performing

RURAL MONTANA — A visitor to Big Sky Country reported today that his mother had enrolled him a Latter-day Saints–sponsored gay program. Allegedly "not a conversion program, and not an ex-gay thing," the program was described as an "intensive camp" that would award one participant a

VW Beetle at the end.

"I flew up from Los Angeles, so I was a little different than most of the participants," the man explained. He reported having two roommates, one of them described as "kind of cocky" and the other "nice." Several women were also part of the program. The camp was described as "hard work" as the participants traveled around the state studying things, working, and performing.

· · · · · ·

Folk singer aids in transcription

Process "laborious"

LOS ANGELES — A well-known folk singer reportedly assisted a local man in transcribing the lyrics to one of his songs so that the man could use it as a teaching tool in an ESL class. The process was allegedly laborious because, as the man explained, "I was typing on my dad's very old computer." The man stated that the task "got frustrating because we were so late."

· · · · · ·

Unprepared for test

LOCAL — Reports tonight indicate that a local man was tasked with administering the GRE history exam in his classroom. The man admits that he hadn't prepared for the test, and at the last minute stated that he was "scrambling" to find a version of the test on the internet.

· · · · · ·

Time-travel excursion

Clover patch admired

NONLOCAL — A man reported today that he was able to travel back in time to the 1950s. Once there, he was allegedly invited to visit a patch of prizewinning clover that was administered by a friend of the man's older brother. The man claimed that he knew this friend would later die in a car wreck.

The man allegedly asked the friend what his name was, and the response was "Locust." The witness expressed his admiration for the clover, and Locust invited him to taste it. Locust subsequently told the man's father that he had sold quite a lot of it.

Unpleasant fashion trend spotted

Woman working Dalmatian look

DOWNTOWN — A local man reported an unsettling fashion trend seen on a downtown street tonight. The man allegedly spotted a woman wearing a white dress with irregular black spots all over it, "like a Dalmatian." When she leaned over, the man stated that the dress had imitation dog testes attached to it, "the size of grapefruits." The witness said several times that the

look was "vulgar."

• • • • • •

Visit to former haunt

Atmosphere "melancholy"

OTTAWA, CANADA — A man reportedly returned to the Canadian capital today "for a visit." As he wandered down Elgin Street, the man reported feeling "melancholy" at remembering the familiar place.

Multiple phone call stress

Relatives "obtuse"

CITY — Frustration was reported tonight by a local man who was receiving too many telephone calls. "Someone kept calling and asking for movie times," the man explained, and both his parents and his sister were allegedly calling separately to ask about his grandmother's financial investments, all the while being "very obtuse." In addition, at the same time someone else was allegedly "trying to send a fax."

· · · · · · ·

Significant events underway

Precision bowling involved

CITY — Something "unbelievably significant is going down," a local man reported tonight. A former work colleague appeared in a parked car "acting all stealthy" in order to deliver "certain invaluable information." The witness alleges that he feels like "I've been interrupted without completing a task" and also that the mission he has been tasked with has something to do precision bowling.

Devil's tail alleged

Roommate "too close"

LOS ANGELES — A man reported tonight that his roommate was changing pants next to him in the backseat of a car, getting too physically close, which "gave me the creeps." The woman allegedly had a cord-like "devil's tail" at the base of her spine, in a bright fleshy color.

· · · · · · ·

Multiple arrests lead to community service

Position refused for disrespect

DOWNTOWN LA — A local man admitted tonight that he was involved in an allegedly illegal caper, but "only as a supporter, not a direct actor." All the participants were reportedly caught and arrested, although one piece of evidence never came to light: the man had been holding, but not using, a stolen credit card.

The principal culprit in the caper was sentenced to community service as a waiter, and the witness reports that he and several others involved in the crime attended an event at a country estate where the waiter was working. The event was allegedly short-staffed, and the man was offered a position as waiter. The manager of the waitstaff and several colleagues came to talk to the man, and the manager, after looking him over, reportedly stated, "Well, I guess we need someone from the middle range." As the group walked to the dressing room where the waitstaff uniforms were kept, the man claims that he asked several others, "Was that a diss?" One of his friends said, "Yes, it was." The man then told the manager, "OK, no, I won't work for you." The manager was reportedly "pissed" but simply brushed the matter off, saying, "Fine."

The witness reported that the manager "said something rude" as the man was leaving. "I just had to have the last word," the man admitted, and pushed his way back through the crowd to where the manager was. The room was reportedly "full of energy," and easily could have devolved into a fight, but the man claims that he kept his cool. Eventually working his way over to the manager, the man told him, "You don't diss someone when you need something from them."

The manager's response was described as "something meaningless" along the lines of "Whatever you say." The witness states that he "let it go," and that three people in his peer group—a man and a woman who were his friends along with another man that he didn't recognize—also decided not to work as waitstaff. The group left to discuss the matter and allegedly to work as waitstaff on their own. When they entered the elevator, they realized it was in the Library Tower on Fifth Street in Downtown Los Angeles.

Stranded abroad without ID

Town "pleasant," has "1970s vibe"

OVERSEAS — A man reports getting stranded overseas today. Initially departing the United States on a train, the man was allegedly traveling with a work colleague. Disembarking in a pleasant river valley, the pair walked to a town, described as clean and crisp and "present," with "a 1970s vibe."

From the town the pair walked up a hill, where the man reports making a cell phone call "to ask for a ride." At that point the man realized that he had no identity documents, air tickets, or other means to get back to the United States.

Sun briefly fades

LOCAL — An area man reported today that the sun temporarily went dark. Describing the effect as "fading out," the man claimed that it lasted "only for a second."

· · · · · ·

Stressful family visit ends at pharmacy

Tic Tac cuisine explored

ARCADIA — Returning to his parents' home today for a visit, a man reported that he was requested to do "a crazy amount" of physical labor. Tasks included carrying several bicycles and moving heavy doors. The experience was described as "stressful"

and allegedly overlapped with concerns about his finances.

One of the man's siblings stated that he was going to visit the man by car for a vacation, and the man subsequently left with a different brother to go shopping at a drugstore. In the shop there were reportedly several booths, "like in a restaurant," where people sat and watched them shopping.

During the checkout process, the two men were joking with the clerk, who inadvertently sprayed spittle on the witness's brother. At the time the man stated that he was eating Tic Tacs and was considering baking a Tic Tac pie.

Teenager requires operation

Persuaded to remain at farm

OTTAWA, CANADA — A visitor to the city reported working with a small group of people on the city's Central Experimental Farm today. One of the group, a teenager with dark hair, allegedly wanted to leave the area, but the others worked to persuade him to stay because he needed an operation.

Hunt for parked car leads to deer hunt

Blood spotted in snow

UP NORTH — Reports today indicate that a man visiting the area spent an inordinate amount of time as a passenger in his brother's car as his sibling allegedly drove around a snowy area trying to determine where the man had parked his own car. The town was described as having curving streets "like a campground."

At one point the men noticed blood in the snow, the result of a deer hunt. A large number of cars were reportedly parked in the area as part of the hunt. The witness stated that he didn't want to look at the blood because "it freaked me out."

· · · · · ·

Terrifying chairlift ride at country estate

Vicious dogs overrun home and yard

UPSTATE NEW YORK — Reports tonight indicate a man's visit to a wealthy family's country estate turned into a terrifying experience. The wealthy family's five daughters were hosting a weekend party in the palatial home, and the man, an invited guest, stated that the house was overrun with dogs, with dog droppings and urine throughout the building. Outside, the base station of the estate's chairlift ride was positioned just beyond the range of a large number of vicious dogs, who were chained to the ground in a line, barking and snarling viciously at people as they boarded the chairlift. Once up in the air on the chairlift and beyond the range of the dogs, the man described the ride as "terrifying" to the point that jumping off seemed like a reasonable solution.

· · · · · ·

Roommates argue, deaths ensue

Full-moon circle held weekly

LOS ANGELES — A man reported getting into a "huge fight" with his roommate today, quickly followed by a series of "terrible things." While fleeing the police a stranger drowned in the pool in the duo's front yard, and in a separate incident, the pair were tasked with breaking the news to a ten-year-old child that his father had died. At the same time, a large party was allegedly going on at the duo's country estate. The man's mother was in attendance, and she invited the other guests to her full-moon circle, held every Saturday in summer "up in the woods."

[*Editor's note:* The full moon occurs about once a month, and thus the week-ly "full-moon circle" described in this story can't be tied to the actual full moon—rather, the name is either symbolic or merely derived from the natural phenomenon.]

• • • • • • •

Old film screened

Man cutting classes "for ages"

CITY — Today reports indicate that a man watched an old 16-mm film at his onetime high school as "private research." The film projector was borrowed from the IT department, and several of the students who worked in the cafeteria kitchen preparing food allegedly joined him to watch the film.

While watching the film, the man stated that he knew he'd missed his class. One of the kitchen workers asked what class he had missed, and the man reportedly replied, "Mrs. H.'s." The student explained then that Mrs. H. had died long before, many months earlier.

The student asked him, "Have you read the letter from England yet?" to which the man admitted that he hadn't. The subsequent question was, "Have you taken the placement test for the new classes yet?" The man reportedly again answered in the negative. He stated that "I'd been cutting class for ages," and then rewound the film.

Lamb barbecue held

Attendees criticized for "overindulgence"

AUSTRALIA — A man reported tonight that he traveled to Australia with three women from a former workplace. The four were invited to a lamb barbecue, and despite claiming that he did not eat meat, the man admitted "I was eating it."

The youngest of the three women left for a moment, and the other two, described as "managers" at the man's former workplace, verbally criticized two businessmen at the barbecue, allegedly claiming that they were "overindulging." The man wasn't part of that conversation, and stated that "I didn't want to hear it."

• • • • • •

New sun "crème" announced

WALL STREET — A major corporation has announced the release of a new sun crème, named Factor 46 Kimberly. From the product label:

"Factor 46 Kimberly is a joke. You should never wear sun crème where you can't splash it, or take off so many clothes that a bird could nip it in the bud and open a whole new can of worms."

House-sitting missteps require special team

Fast, quiet new helicopter tech employed

OUT WEST — Hired to house-sit for a Taiwanese military family, a local man admits to being red-faced tonight. The terms of the house-sitting agreement were reportedly that the house had to be in the same condition when the family returned as when they had left, but the man stated that "We had played in there, and partied."

The man and his roommate had been flown out to the country house by the military, in a purported "new type" of helicopter that flew fast and very quietly. Before the family returned to the house, a special team was dispatched to put everything back in exactly the condition it had been in before.

Subsequently invited back to the house for a church picnic, the man stated that he was "deeply embarrassed" at his own behavior in front of all the military people.

Mathematical solution found

Mother seething

SAN FRANCISCO — Reports tonight indicate that a man's mother is currently staying in the City by the Bay and "seething with anger." She had allegedly planned a party for someone's birthday. The man stated that "I've got it all figured out mathematically" and claimed he knew what to do, as well as how to do it. With his confidence allegedly boosted by a recent hookup, the man had insights into what he termed "the next phase." He clarified that the hookup was "a representative of the process, not an instigator."

· · · · · ·

Fruitless quest for parking

Mock fistfight in café

IN A SMALL TOWN — A visitor to the area reported today that he drove around a small town for some time in search of a street parking space. He allegedly intended to leave his car so that he could take the train, but all the parking signs stated that parking was restricted until 11:30 p.m. Finally the man drove across the tracks and parked at a café.

A rotund man at the café turned out to be an old friend, and the witness alleges that "he sucker-punched me." The witness responded in kind, and then the two shared a hug. Other people in the café reportedly realized at that moment that it wasn't a real fistfight. The two men left the café and walked toward the train station.

On returning to the town, the man reportedly discovered a note left on his windshield. His broth-er had written the note for the parking enforcement officer, a personal friend of the brother, asking her not to issue a citation for the vehicle.

Complex wiring repairs attempted

Four lines for "secure redundancy"

CITY — A man reported tonight that he attempted to fix the wiring in the family home before he had to leave. The man admitted that he had built "shoddy" phone-wire connectors that were all loose. Some of the wires were in sets of four running over the nearby mountains. Although only one wire was needed, the man alleged that running four wires created "secure redundancy." With his family in the

house, the man attempted to match the colors of various wires in a complex series of wire connectors.

· · · · · ·

Man bilocates, overhears gossip

Moped rider "looking for stuff to steal"

LOS ANGELES — Walking home through the Hollywood neighborhood, a local man reported that it was "so late and so dark" that he phoned his roommate and asked for a ride. The roommate responded that he would try to come later on.

While walking home the man alleged that he was bilocating: in addition to treading the streets of Hollywood he was also on the sofa in his childhood home, where he allegedly overheard family members talking about him.

In Hollywood a moped reportedly drove past the man, moving slowly and with its lights off. The man feared that the driver was attempting to menace him, but it turned out that he was simply looking in cars for things to steal.

At his childhood home, the man snuck out the back door, allegedly finding it in the wrong place, and walked up the road to the top of a hill. He stated that he spotted his father's small white pickup turn into a neighboring gate, but the man claimed that he was focused on trying to return to his body on the streets of Hollywood.

• • • • • •

Quest for night javelin space

Condo residents oblivious to interlopers

SUBURBIA — Reports indicate that a man and his friend spent the night "running all over" a condominium complex. "We went right through many of the condo units," the man claimed, "even though there were people in them. They didn't notice." The two men discussed the HOA fees of the complex on their quest to find some open space for the witness's friend to practice with his javelin in the dark.

Woman assaults offspring

Frailty minimizes injury

CITY — A local man reported that his mother verbally and physically assaulted him tonight. "I had mixed something up that embarrassed her," the man alleged. In the man's bedroom the woman shouted at him and then "hit me in the face." The man explained that "I wasn't afraid, because she was frail. But it was emotional."

Film depicts secret attack boat

Liquid rubber employed for repairs

LOS ANGELES — Reports today state that a local man has been hired to repair the rubber pontoons used in a war movie. The man claims that he was tasked with making the repairs using liquid rubber.

The film features a prominent television actor in command of a secret attack boat. The character is depicted at various ages by members of the same family of actors.

· · · · · ·

Frustrating terminal search

GREAT BRITAIN — Reports today indicate that a man trying to catch a flight at a British airport was actually at the wrong terminal. Knowing that he was likely going to miss his flight, he wandered the airport's corridors looking for his departure gate, even stepping outside into the snow. The man described the experience as "frustrating."

· · · · · ·

Neighbors interrupt dinner

Tenant disbelieves eviction rumor

CITY — A dinner party was interrupted tonight when several neighbors of a local man dropped in to console him. The neighbors allegedly expressed their sympathy that the man had been evicted from the house. "I thought it was a joke, or a rumor," the man stated, "and I sent them away." Subsequently the man found an eviction letter under his doormat, and reported feeling angry that news of his eviction had spread before he'd ever heard about it.

Shoemaking machine disrupts commuter rail line

Water tournament organized

UPSTATE AND WEST HOLLY-WOOD, CALIF. — Working as a camp counsellor this summer, a man reported that "there was lots of swimming." The man organized a water tournament with other participants, including a former work colleague, in a large pool.

The man reports that a historic story came up about a French official who used a tall machine that manufactured shoes, connecting the leather upper to the sole. The

machine was described as "dangerous" because it extended through the overhead wires of the West Hollywood light-rail line. At one point the witness stated that the machine became entangled in the train's pantograph and got thrown into the large pool.

Reunion features 1970s threads

Greeting song performed

THE COUNTRYSIDE — Two families were reportedly reunited this summer for the first time in many years. A man described the other participants as dressed in 1970s clothing in "bright, fun" colors.

One of the children, a boy approximately twelve years old and wearing a tweed hat, allegedly an-nounced that his "friend from Canada" had taught him how to sing a greeting, and proceeded to perform the song. The child called the man "my favorite see" meaning his favorite uncle.

The man claimed that the event, held in a grassy area, was "light, sunny, and happy."

Man admits psychotherapy work

Hitler's mistress "always" wore mask

WARTIME GERMANY — A man reports tonight that he worked as the psychotherapist for one of Hitler's mistresses. The man stated that "she always wore a gas mask," and that near the end of the war, the Fuhrer was followed everywhere by clouds of gas in order to protect him.

At one point the woman removed the gas mask while aboard a ship, and then put it on again for the journey back to rejoin Hitler in what was described as his "stadium headquarters." The man explained that "there was even a World War II–era song, in German, about the gas."

Unique office lamp

CITY — A local man reports that the office he rented, at a cost of $1,000 per month, was "more like a dorm room." The office had a lamp that was described as a long, straight pipe with a bulb at the top, with adjustable height. The man stated that he flexed the lamp stand out to its maximum reach to illuminate his bed, which was positioned "higher up."

· · · · · ·

Sex-club excursion leads to gas station damage

Note left under wiper

LAS VEGAS — A visitor to Sin City reported tonight that he had been "going to sex clubs" but found the experience less than satisfactory. He planned to go to one more club by car, and got into his car at a casino parking lot. A note had allegedly been left under his wiper, but the man stated that "I just drove away."

The man then learned that the vehicle had been left "for hours" at a casino gas station, and he drove away with the nozzle still in his gas tank, breaking it off and dragging the hose behind the vehicle. This set off alarms, and he stopped and exited the vehicle.

As the gas station crew were cleaning up the damage, the man allegedly spotted his keys near the gas cap. "Some mechanical flaw had allowed me to drive the car without the key in the ignition," he reported.

Lamb languages, planets discovered

Influence on development of human languages

PLANET EARTH — Reports tonight indicate that in the future, a man overhears two people talking about lamb languages and lamb planets. The discovery of these planets—where the alien inhabitants look like lambs—influenced the development of some human languages on Earth.

The grammatical structure, which developed mostly in African languages, involved placing a word for the person you're speaking to at the beginning of each sentence.

The two individuals that the man overheard were inside a capsule that was to be dropped in free

fall to achieve an as yet unspecified goal regarding lamb languages. The individuals reportedly discussed "some other topic" that would alter the outcome of the capsule drop and obviate the lamb-language work.

• • • • • •

Promised swank disappoints

LOCAL — A European woman reportedly invited three locals out tonight for a "swanky dinner." One of the guests reported that the promised upscale dining establishment "was just the cafeteria at the university."

• • • • • •

"Creative types" host orgy

LOS ANGELES — Reports tonight indicate that a local man was staying at the apartment of some friends, described as "wild and creative types." A knock at the door turned out to be a group of people who had arrived to participate in an orgy.

Heated battle in defense of White House

Svena described as heroic

WASHINGTON, D.C. — A man reports working as "an agent" in defense of the White House during a heated melee that involved hand-to-hand combat with bombs, razors, and other weapons. "One of my colleagues got blown up to save me," the man alleges. One of the heroes among the group of secret agents was a woman named Svena, described as having black hair. The man reported that the fighting included swordplay, and "we were sleeping on sofas, like in an emergency."

At one point a group of children broke into the building, and the man was reportedly forced to tell them "I'm serious." He allegedly nicked the forehead of one of the children so quickly that the child didn't see it happen, and the child found a drop of blood on their forehead afterward. This caused the children to finally take the matter seriously.

A combatant wearing a gas mask launched a mini bomb into the room using a wire rail. The weapon was described as "like a marble." Someone allegedly shouted "Hit the deck," and all those present did so except the partner of the reporting witness, who held the door closed so that the bomber couldn't enter.

Subsequently the man described feeling "painless" in the quiet darkness. Someone reportedly scratched the man's feet and legs "to make sure I could feel them."

Kiss stolen at party

LOCAL — A man reported attending a party tonight at which a friend of a friend surreptitiously kissed him. The other man was described as "blond" and "cute." The witness alleged that later, the man crawled into his bed, "but just for a moment."

Highball margarita order error

LOS ANGELES — A local man reported tonight that he was in a bar with a former roommate. Asked for his drink order, the man allegedly said, "a highball margarita." The woman then said, "But you don't drink." The man responded, "Oh, right," and revised his order.

• • • • • •

Office workers wear same costume

LOS ANGELES — A local office worker reported that "a lot of people" at his office had dressed up in the same costume for Halloween today. The costume was described as "shirtless, with some tattoos."

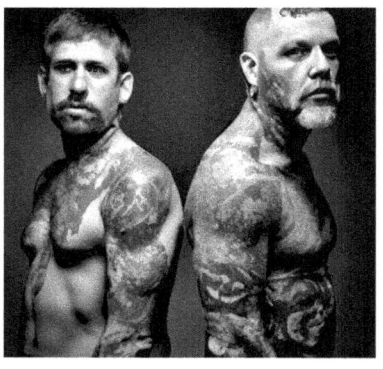

Fountain crash reveals concealed void

LOCAL — A local man reported today that he was riding a cart along a polished stone track in a fountain. When the cart struck the wall at the back of the fountain, a tiled wall allegedly collapsed, and water coursed downward, flooding the space below. The man stated that the people who had concealed this void were "upset."

• • • • • •

Translation required for meeting in bar

English speaker struggles with Japanese, French

PARIS — A visitor to the city reported tonight that he has been acting as a guide and translator for two Japanese women. The group was slated to meet three people in a bar—a man and two women, one of whom was German.

The witness claimed that he entered the bar alone at first to explain that he was acting as the translator. In speaking to the staff, the man reported that he inadvertently used the *tu* form of the French verbs, then belatedly asked the staff for permission to use such informal language.

When he spoke to the lo-cal meeting attendees, the man stated that the older of the two local women, the German, "said something perfunctory about Canada" before he asked the Japanese women to enter and join the group. The man translated the first question from the Japanese delegates: "Will the export numbers for France be the same as for Germany next year?"

The German woman allegedly "had to mull it over" before responding. The local trio then left the bar "to see someone off" but promised that they would be right back.

• • • • • •

Dogs host humans on straw beds

NEARBY — A man report-ed today that people and dogs were "hanging out" on straw beds, with the ca-nines described as "quite feral." The humans were said to be guests on the straw beds, which were home to a canine society.

• • • • • •

Track marks visible through shirt

Fabric "sheer"

DOWNTOWN LOS ANGELES — At a loft party downtown tonight, a local resident alleged he saw a man at the party who was wearing "a sheer blue-and-white shirt." The individual was described as "nervous" that someone would see his track marks. The witness explains that he spotted the track marks under the man's shirt, on his inner arms. Rather than attempting to hide them, the witness stated, the man was simply covering them up for the party.

Cable car ride characterized by too much luggage

SAN FRANCISCO — A visitor to the city described riding a cable car today, alleging that he and his traveling companion both "had too much luggage." The man stated that he was waiting for the car to stop so that he could join his companion at a café.

Man rewarded with cliff seat

View "just for me"

LOS ANGELES — Reports tonight indicate that a local man has achieved a state of mind recommended by a local *dō* master. [*Editor's note:* The term *dō* (道) relates to a variety of East Asian philosophical, religious, and martial fields, including Taoism and *budō* martial arts. Broadly, the term implies a "path" or "way of life."]

As a reward for achieving this state, the man was allegedly allowed to sit on top of a high cliff overlooking the city. The man stated that he'd seen the *dō* master sitting in the same place. The view from the cliff was reportedly "just for me," and included a park, a "geometrically perfect" traffic circle, and a college campus with many red buildings.

· · · · · ·

Faulty headlights lead to graveyard visit

LOS ANGELES — Allegedly due to the fact that the lights on his car "weren't really working," a local man attempted to stop at a garage tonight, pulling into a parking space behind a building. In the area were many ancient statues and gravestones, but the man reports that he was able to avoid hitting any of them. Because daybreak was imminent, he was able to stop worrying about the malfunctioning lights.

Archaeologists uncover onions

Condition "filthy"

LOS ANGELES — A local man and his high school friend allegedly purchased salad ingredients today at a local store. The green onions were described as "extremely dirty." The pair made the salad in the store, and then made coffee.

Several hundred years later, archaeologists dug up the green onions in the detritus of a stove, and managed to date the remains based on this very journalistic report.

Man ditched in Rhode Island

Watches skiing with local

PROVIDENCE, R.I. — A California man reportedly moved to the city today along with two college-era friends. After making the lengthy trip by car, the man got separated from his companions in the student center. Unable to locate them, the man allegedly inquired at the desk, and the clerk stated that her records showed that the two had gone to Cleveland, Ohio, and not to Providence. The clerk stated that the pair had a "small white fox terrier" with them. The man had met the dog and thus accepted the clerk was talking about the same people.

Realizing that he'd been "ditched," the man walked around the residential part of the city, reporting that the "huge hulking apartment blocks" were "dirty, like in Warsaw."

The man found himself using an old woman's bathroom, and she came in to discover him there, but in the man's words, "she was cool." The woman served him buns, and the pair sat in her bed talking. When the woman's husband came home, he was accompanied by a young couple, and the trio looked in at the witness and his host from the hallway. The witness similarly described woman's husband as "cool."

From the bed the pair watched skiers descending a distant hill. Described as "like a vast industrial project," the woman insisted that it wasn't, but rather was a natural formation.

• • • • • •

Steep cost to borrow garbage truck

Nausea-inducing trash

PALM SPRINGS, CALIF. — At the municipal dump in the desert city, located on a sandy hill overlooking the town, a man and several friends asked to borrow a garbage truck. They were told they could use a garbage truck if they helped unload it. The group set to work, and in the truck found what the witness described as "slaughterhouse remains." The gore caused some members of the group to "barf." Among the remains was a side of beef described as "still twitching" as well as a goat kid, which jumped out of the truck and ran away.

Club outing thwarted

Bad dye job blamed

OTTAWA, CANADA — A man visiting the city reported going to a nightclub with a couple of men and a couple of women. The club was located in a beautiful part of the city, which the witness compared to Paris. The group was denied entry to the nightclub because they hadn't signed in on the guest list, and also because one of the women had what was described as "a poor dye job." The witness stated that her highlights were "OK" but not dyed very well.

On exiting the club, the man stated that he went out to the street alone because one of the men in the group had allegedly forgotten his camera at the club, and the others had all gone back to retrieve it. From the street the man reported being "amazed" that the club had been on the fifteenth floor, and realized that was why he had been able to view the adjacent church spire so clearly from the environs of the club.

As he waited for the others in the group, the man watched people in the alley behind a restaurant packing up boxes of food. When the others finally joined him, the group reportedly walked to nearby Government Square, where the buildings were all lit from outside.

Tornado stalks French train

*Complex parking structure
lit with fractals*

PARIS — A visitor to the French capital reported taking a late-night train ride in the country with his brother, who sat one seat ahead of him. The man reported that he had his briefcase with him, and when the train got nearer to Paris, daylight broke, and they were in his own neighborhood again. Rail lines and an airport were nearby, in an area described as

"south of the city."

From the train the men watched cargo jets taking off, and a train with big equipment on it going under the highway and then becoming a bus. A violent tornado reportedly appeared in the fields on the right side, described as "moving fast and nearby." The man alleges that a group of English-speakers were sitting in front of him, engrossed in conversation and unaware of the risk, and he warned them: "Tornado."

Later, at the Paris airport, the man reported searching a huge "parking tree" structure because he was flying out to the Mediterranean in the morning. The man reports noting that it was 9:30 p.m., but the tree structure was scheduled to close at 11 p.m. The facility was described as bathed in "neat" lights in blue and white fractal patterns that spun very fast. Staffers indirectly signaled the man to come down, and he subsequently talked to a police officer and the facility's operator. "There was no hassle," the man explained, "and I asked for help to find my car."

. . . . . .

Teacher runs late

Unprepared for class

LOCAL — A local resident reported today that he was running late for a class he was slated to teach. Making his tardiness worse was the fact that he'd missed the previous class altogether. Once the class started, the man allegedly took one of the students out of the classroom in order to discuss his lottery win, at which point several other students left the class.

During the class the man stated that he was unable to find the right page number in the textbook, and he'd forgotten to grade the class's homework assignments. A British comedian dropped in on the class and allegedly wiped his orange lollipop on the hem of the man's toga. The witness complained that he was going to have go wash it out in the men's room sink.

. . . . . .

Doll bakes with cookies

Pink yogurt key ingredient

LOS ANGELES — Reportedly perfecting a cookie recipe that he wanted to put into mass production, a local man enlisted the help of acquaintance with an oven. Exact details of the recipe were not revealed, but a major ingredient was said to be pink yogurt.

While the two men were baking sample cookies, a small doll got into the oven along with the dough. The doll allegedly shouted to be let out, and when the baking process was finished, she emerged with much darker skin and was described as "not happy about it." The witness stated that the doll didn't feel pain from being baked, but believed that she had already been dark enough.

· · · · · · ·

Unexpected appearance of sibling

Meeting disrupted

LOS ANGELES — An all-hands office meeting was reportedly interrupted today by the appearance of the brother of one of the office staff. The man stated that he briefly left the meeting and gave his brother his keys and his cell phone. On returning to the meeting, he allegedly cracked a joke about "strangling" his sibling.

· · · · · · ·

Wrong door handle locked

Punks sort mail

LONDON — A California man reported tonight that he was staying with his sister at the home of a friend in the British capital. Despite being given explicit instructions to the contrary, the man locked both the deadbolt and the handle of the door. The homeowner had no key for the lock on the handle. On closer examination, however, it allegedly turned out to be a simple mailbox lock assembly that was easy to dismantle.

The homeowner's mail was there in the parking garage, and the man reported that "some punks" went through the mail and disposed of the junk mail. The man alleged that he didn't have time to check their work, and asked the punks for the homeowner's letters, but they were already in a "sticky wet trash bag." The man described driving out of the garage, and subsequently encountering a truckload of laborers that wouldn't let him merge.

· · · · · ·

Carpet turned into coasters

Nails removed from thread lattice

WEST HOLLYWOOD, CALIF. — Pulling out the lattice of crisscrossing threads by removing the nails used to hold the lattice in place, a local man tonight explained that he is disassembling what he described as "an old green carpet" in order to make

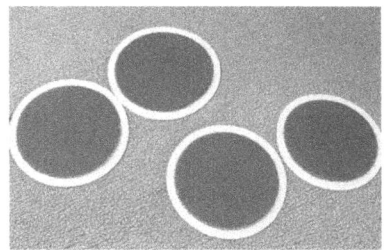

circular coasters.

· · · · · ·

Bank form sought

Slow progress in arena search

TOKAI REGION, JAPAN — A local resident reported slowly searching a sports complex tonight with a woman. The alleged target was the correct form needed to pay a bill owed to the bank. The man found a copy of the form, and mistakenly filled in the wrong amount, and so had to continue searching for another copy.

A marathon race was scheduled for later in the day, and the pair stepped outside the stadium to eat fried chicken with other people who were waiting for the race to begin. The man stated that everyone eventually joined in the marathon race, and later sat around an outdoor *kotatsu,* "chatting amiably." [*Editor's note:* in Japan a *kotatsu* (炬燵) is a low wooden table with a heater under it, covered by a heavy blanket, to keep people warm on cold winter evenings.]

New bullet train technology revealed

Shinkansen "light" on its rails

TOKAI REGION, JAPAN — A visitor to the country reported running through a train station to catch the "new, light" shinkansen bullet train. Explaining the new technology, the man stated that the train "was light on its rails." The station was described as "darkish," and when he finally found the correct platform, some high

school colleagues were allegedly waiting there to say good-bye.

· · · · · ·

Terrorist school takeover

Elevator delays hamper arrival

LOCAL — An area resident today reported that "terrorists" had taken over his school, so he obtained a handgun, and loaded it, "and was walking around with it." He stated that he and other teachers took the parking elevator down, rather than the regular elevator, and were thus late.

· · · · · ·

Intercity train ride

Irish visitors pore over maps

LOS ANGELES — A local man reported riding a train today between two California cities along with a college friend. Also in the rail car with them were a group of Irish people, an older male-female couple and a young woman, who were allegedly using a laptop printer to print maps of Japan.

The man alleges that he showed the group a map of the western Kanto region, and examined a larger map, then advised the group that they should visit Itakone. The younger woman had a 3-D pop-up map book, and the witness stated that he began to write out directions on how the Irish trio could take the train up the Oi River in order to see "the old Japan."

The train then pulled into the station at Fukuroi in Shizuoka Prefecture, where many people boarded and disembarked. The man stated that his college friend might have disembarked at this stop, but he wasn't certain whether he himself should.

· · · · · ·

Attacked by interdimensional invisible beings

Kappa summoned

LOS ANGELES — A local man claims tonight that he has been attacked by invisible beings. "They were biting me," the man explained, "especially in one stairwell of my apartment building." After some effort, the man allegedly could start to see them. The beings were described as "interdimensional demons or ghosts."

With the help of several friends, the man concocted a set of special lenses so that other people could see the beings the same way that he did. The group reported walking through a large party, where the man pointed out "all the dead."

When the group reached a bench in front of a fountain on a shopping street, they saw that one of the man's former coworkers had knocked a large ghoul into the water. The bench was reportedly still broken from when the witness had been attacked there. The witness asked the ghoul, "Was it you who attacked me here?" The ghoul nodded in response, but the man noticed that it had a broken tooth, which was its way of summoning a *kappa*. The man told his former coworker and friends to "walk away nonchalantly" because "we don't want to mess with a *kappa*." The man explained that if they saw the creature, they should not look it in the eye. He then saw, "from the corner of my eye," a *kappa* stepping out of the water across the street. The man stated that "at the last moment, one of the group looked at it."

[*Editor's note:* the *kappa* (河童) is a turtle-like river-dwelling creature from Japanese folklore. Fond of cucumbers and wrestling, they can be both friendly and dangerous to humans.]

Magazine freelance work

Page proofs incomplete, error-ridden

LOCAL — An area resident reportedly took a job freelancing for a conservative Canadian print magazine. The magazine offices were conveniently located directly across the hall from the man's apartment. A magazine staffer, described as "a big woman," allegedly brought page proofs to the man's apartment. "The text wasn't all there yet," the man explained, and the document "had color and contrast problems." Stating that he was unsure whether the woman was aware of the issues, or whether she planned to fix them or not, he informed her of the problems.

· · · · · ·

Neighbors remembered

Secret crushes revealed

LOCAL — When querying his parents regarding some long-ago neighbors, a local man learned some disturbing details. The man described the neighbors as a family that lived nearby, "where the Petersons live now," when he was in early childhood. The man stated that the family name was Mardison, and remembers the father as "very good looking."

When queried, his parents revealed that "the little girl in the family was in love with you" and had lived in three different houses waiting for the man to act. The man asserts that "I didn't know."

The man then remembered the son in fami-ly, allegedly named Jody, and realized he would be grown now and was probably good-looking. He planned to look for the man in case he might be a good dating prospect.

Looking at his face in the bathroom mirror, the man reportedly realized it wasn't really his face— the eyes were narrow, and the shape of the face more feminine.

Dog confronts gorillas

Great apes living near LA supermarket

LOS ANGELES — Reports tonight indicate that a local man's German shepherd was growling at several gorillas that were living in trees outside a supermarket. The man's husband allegedly shouted at the dog to "stand down." The witness reports that one of the gorillas was "glaring" at the dog.

Correction fluid ineffective

Excursion halted by hotel activity

SAN FRANCISCO — Reports today indicate that a local man got a phone call that led him to fill out a form on behalf of his father. While trying to correct the form using Wite-Out correction fluid, the man stated that the fluid was too thin, and then the brush broke; "It was a mess." Finally the man realized he could simply print out another copy of the form from the Web.

The phone call also led the man to take a drive with his brother around San Francisco. Stating that his brother was driving, the pair eventually got stuck on a street where a hotel was using all the lanes to unload newly arriving guests.

. . . . . .

Forced to fold sweaters

OVERSEAS — A man reported tonight that he boarded a flight to a foreign destination, where he was "forced to work in a factory folding sweaters with everybody else."

. . . . . .

Office worker preps in restroom

Purpose of meeting murky

LOS ANGELES — A local resident reports today that he spent time preparing for a meeting in the office restroom while the meeting's other participant was waiting. "I had to prepare him for an upcoming event," the man explained, "and I had to ingratiate myself with him."

The man stated that the meeting was "important" and that the "true matter" would come up later on, but he denied knowing what the matter was.

. . . . . .

Family home rearranged

Siblings change names, rooms

THE OLD HOMETOWN — A man reportedly returned to this family home for a visit this week and stated that he had to sleep on the floor while other family members were having breakfast. The man's father asked his older brother, "So what do you do, Gordon?" even though his brother's name wasn't

Gordon. Much to his surprise, his brother answered the question.

Also present was the man's nephew, who allegedly complained about the food he had to eat. A list of the nephew's food rules was reportedly tattooed on his torso.

An unknown room had allegedly been added to the house, described as "on the northeast side." People that the man didn't know were reportedly "moving stuff out of it." His sister's bedroom had been completely rearranged, with a smaller bed, and the man overheard other family members refer to it as "mom's room." He reportedly tried to explain to others present that the room had always been his sister's bedroom.

· · · · · ·

Subway exit leads to Mojave Desert

Westside street a direct link

NEW YORK CITY — Admitting that he was "slacking" on some contracts at his company in the Garment Center district in the Big Apple's Manhattan borough, a local man said he left the area by subway with his cousin. While his cousin stayed on the train, the man exited the subway "somewhere in the West

40s" and began walking west. The street reportedly led him directly into the Mojave Desert.

Money missing on hike

IN THE WOODS — A man stated today that he went for a hike in the forest with his GPS receiver in hand. Although he started the hike alone, he soon found himself in the company of "a dangerous guy and his girlfriend," but stated that the guy was actually a friend.

The man alleged that

"we were watching a mystery on television, but we were also living it." The mystery allegedly concerned a great deal of money that goes missing after being hidden in the friend's pickup truck. The friend reportedly didn't know who had taken the money, but the witness stated that "I suspected it was his girlfriend."

The friend then drove the man to a small regional airport to catch a flight.

Expanded gardens visited

Toad, tomatoes placed in blender

TOKAI REGION, JAPAN — Reports today state that a man visiting the area called at the home of a former employer. The woman's estate now covered many acres, with sprawling outdoor gardens and drainage ditches, with "little bridges" spanning the ditches.

The woman and her husband were there working on the greenery, and the witness reported that he was asked to put a dead toad into the blender with several tomatoes. The witness also stated "that weird neighbor couple was around."

New bridge at Liffey estuary

Waves wash over structure

DUBLIN, IRELAND — The Irish capital has a new bridge tonight, spanning the Liffey estuary. The new structure was described as approximately 1,100 yards long and "right along the seafront." Pedestrians walking along the previous shore path often got washed over by waves. The new structure, however, described as "more

of a low causeway," isn't much higher—pedestrians walking on the bridge also experience waves washing over them.

Books dropped in mud

Anger at high schoolers

LOS ANGELES — In the Fairfax District tonight a man reported carrying four books that he had just purchased and inadvertently dropping two of them in a mud puddle. A high-school student unintentionally stepped on the books, and the man stated that he "reacted angrily." The student's friends verbally criticized the man, and he allegedly walked away.

At the sink in front of the large atrium window at Canter's Deli, the man reportedly stopped to wash off the muddied books. The quartet of high school students allegedly sat nearby at an outdoor table, further raising the man's ire.

• • • • • • •

Wrong photo on ID

Traffic stop uncovers error

LOS ANGELES — Stopped at a random police checkpoint tonight, a local man stated that the officers discovered the photo on his ID wasn't his photo but rather a photo of former president Ronald Reagan. The photo matched one found later in the document.

The man stated that he blamed the new 1984 security state and the economic recession, and then "burst into tears." The police instructed him to go to the passport office next door. His family reportedly gathered later a Trader Joe's supermarket to have dinner.

Mementos retrieved

Apartment moved into hotel room

NARITA, JAPAN — A former resident of the island nation reportedly returned today to clean out his old apartment, only to discover that it had all been moved into a hotel room near Narita Airport. The man reported packing up knickknacks, cups, books, a bronze figure his grandmother had fired, along with pottery, packing everything into his backpack.

The man stated that a work colleague from Los Angeles was present, but that he was on another flight, and the man had little time to interact with him because "I was late."

• • • • • •

Aerial dogfights down under

AUSTRALIA — A visitor to the southern nation stated that he participated in several "dogfights" with local pilots in military aircraft.

"I was also riding a school bus," the man explained, "and at one point I forgot my bag on the bus."

• • • • • •

Backstreet "square" named after pope
Jovial pontiff appears riding unicycle

HOLLYWOOD, CALIF. — Local officials this morning dedicated a public square, described by a journalist as "more of a backstreet intersection, really," to incoming pope Benedict XVI, affectionately known in the area as "Ratzi." Ceremonies included erecting a street sign with the new pope's name and photo on it, although traffic on the cross streets was not halted. "Ratzi was there with the pointy hat and everything," one eyewitness claimed. "He was acting really happy, and riding around on a unicycle."

The location of the

newly anointed square is at 34° 5′ 59″ north latitude, 118° 20′ 52″ west longitude (34.0997453, -118.3478972).

• • • • • • •

Man evades new police state authorities

Kindergarten ruse

LOCAL — An area resident reported tonight that a new police state was in effect, and "many people are poor." The man alleges that he had to "hide in the open" in order to evade imprisonment.

While the man was in his mother's kindergarten class, an inspector, described as "a child," came to verify the identities of the participants. The man reported that he was forced to sit in a circle with the children "on those little-kid chairs," but that it worked—the inspector questioned his identity but didn't turn him in.

• • • • • •

Church detective work

ATLANTA — A man reported today that he was hired to work as a detective at a local church. He also claimed that the pastor's son "refused to date detectives."

• • • • • •

Mystery of missing woman deepens

Phone difficulties; fuel truck burns

PAPUA NEW GUINEA — Reports tonight indicate an ongoing conspiracy at a big hotel in Papua New Guinea. A visitor to the Southeast Asian nation related the evening's events. The man described "snooping around" the Grand Hotel with an acquaintance that he occasionally hooked up with. While in the stairwell of the hotel, the man alleged that they "overheard something."

A few miles down the beach, a hotel waitress reportedly disappeared from a small café. The man claimed that he and his hookup attempted to find out what had happened to the woman, "but we were stonewalled." The café owner, described as a middle-age woman, gave them her permission to use the café's telephone, and the man attempted to dial out, "but I kept screwing it up," as the old rotary telephone was "too confusing."

A local expat then reportedly loaned the man his cell phone. He placed a call to someone back at the hotel who was "about to reveal something" when "we almost got cut off." At that point, the hotel's security chief arrived, and went into the missing woman's room, and returned with a fuel-carry-

ing semitrailer truck. "We were supposed to think he'd been kidnapped," the witness explained, "but someone knew that he'd staged it." The fuel truck subsequently crashed and caught fire. The witness reported that he went into a corner where some of his clothes were scattered around, and a high-school

era acquaintance loaded the clothes into her new backpack when the man left.

Much overtime at apartment-based job

Multiple beds reduce rent

CITY — Working a job described as "in an apartment," a local man reported working "a lot" of overtime because "there's nothing else to do." His sister reportedly also

works there, but she allegedly leaves at 5 p.m.

Walking into the back rooms, the man stated that he discovered a friend from childhood sleeping in a bed. The woman had placed a second bed in each of the bedrooms, which the man acknowledged was a clever way to reduce her own rental costs.

In the other bedroom the man found a small bound book that several people were allegedly using as a journal. Among those who had made entries were his sister, his brother, and the driver of his school bus route from many years earlier. The man stated that he read the entries that had been written by his siblings.

· · · · · ·

Visit to agent's office thwarted

Passersby delay elevator

LOS ANGELES — Reporting that he had received a letter from a casting agent about a potential film role, a local man stated that he visited the agent's office to discuss the matter. The guard at the building, described as "very rude," allegedly wouldn't let him in, nor would he inform the casting agent of his presence.

The man stated that he then shredded the letter and threw the pieces around the lobby. Other people then wouldn't let his elevator car go down, allegedly repeatedly blocking the door. The man stated that he attempted to push them out of the elevator car, and that "they wanted to call the cops," but eventually the elevator door closed.

· · · · · ·

New neighborhood airport

Owners morals questioned

LOCAL — Driving through his childhood neighborhood with his parents and two nephews in what was described as "a heavy truck," a man reported that a neighbor had opened a new business. The neighbor had set up an airport with "several of his own planes" as well as a $19.95 tie-down fee.

The witness's parents implied that this new

business was an infringement on something they were doing. The man's mother allegedly said that the neighbor had once "screwed over" his father. When pressed for details, she stated that the neighbor had promised to eliminate pests in the yard and instead had given everyone a disease.

The family stopped at a restaurant, and the man alleged that his father went in ahead of the others for a few minutes in order to talk to the airport-owning neighbor.

The owner of the restaurant placed flowers in each meal served, "even in winter," and the witness stated that there were two German tourists in the restaurant who were "very happy with their lunches." The man's mother stated that the restaurant owner did all her own canning, which was "a lot of work."

· · · · · ·

Dog atop parking structure

Wrong animal descends escalator

NEW YORK CITY — A visitor to the city reported today that his dog, a black German shepherd, was sitting atop an urban parking garage. When the witness went into the structure, the wrong dog—a small terrier—came down the escalator. The man's husband was reportedly angry, and the pair visited the facility manager's of-

fice. The manager was described as "indifferent" to the issue.

· · · · · ·

Back way found impassible

Fruitless quest for laundry

LOCAL — Returning home after a stint at summer camp, a man reports finding his parents and brother staying at a hotel. As they left the hotel on foot, the man called after them "for the car keys," so that he could check whether his jeans were still at the laundry next door. The man stated that he'd left his jeans there before he'd gone to camp.

The man reported that he found his white shirt in the car and that it had been dry-cleaned; he described his reaction as, "How thoughtful." Driving toward the hotel, the man stated that he took a back way, through rough and rocky terrain and off-road. Eventually the man was forced to turn around because the path was "too rough."

Man caught in underpants at murder trial

Event "more like performance"

LOS ANGELES — In the courthouse where Anna Nicole Smith's murder trial was being held, a local man stated that he was wearing "only my underwear" as he tried to find the courtroom and join several friends who were in attendance. Eventually the man found the right balcony at the venue, then reportedly realized that his friends were on the left balcony.

The trial was described as "more like a performance," with entertainment during the intermission.

Recipe class derailed

Substitute ingredients sought at market

SINGAPORE — A class was taught in the city today by a man hired to elucidate a recipe that had appeared in the newspaper. During the class, when he got to the end of the instruc- tions, the man discovered that they would need to kill and skin some ground squirrels to obtain their fatty meat.

Instead, the man went to a local market, accompanied by what he described as "the best student" to obtain marbled beef as a substitute. Afterward, the class was scheduled to analyze the food in terms of culture and language.

The market was reportedly inside a cinema, and the street outside was described as "crowded with tourists." The man stated that his student companion "was happy" and that the woman "had such an eclectic range of things to do in her life."

· · · · · ·

Shipboard surf lessons

PACIFIC OCEAN — While aboard a ship, a man reported watching a famous Hollywood actor teach surfing lessons. One of the female students allegedly arrived on a motorized surfboard.

Prison conspiracy reported by class scofflaw

High-rise office break-in

OTKI AND NEW YORK CITY — "A conspiracy," a local man reported, is underway tonight at Otki Prison, adding that "There are scary goings-on." The man explained that he was snuck into the first-class dining room from the main dining room by a steward. The man's motivation for this subterfuge was allegedly that "A man in there saw me on the street and wanted a date with me."

Later, in the Empire State Building, the man

reported that he quickly tried to get dressed as the alarms went off. Claiming to be British, he was said to be wearing heavy British winter clothes.

Afterward, explaining to journalists that his twin brother was breaking in to an office somewhere upstairs, the witness stated that he managed to casually chat with the police as he left the building.

Too "scattered" to catch train

Famous singer spotted

KAKEGAWA, JAPAN — A visitor to the area reported today that he was at the train station attempting to catch the bullet train. The man reported that his state of mind was not conducive to the task, describing himself as "scattered" and "my bags were everywhere." The man stated that as a result, he was forced to wait for the next train several times.

Also at the Kakegawa station was a well-known American chanteuse, famous for pop music in the 1960s and 1970s, but the witness stated that she wasn't there to catch the train.

Bikini boutique robbery thwarted

Laptop recovered, dictionary broken

MEXICO — On a holiday with a former roommate, a man reports that his traveling companion went into a boutique to try on "very expensive" Rosa Chá bikinis. The owner of the shop showed the man documentation of a financial dispute she'd had with the former editor of a U.S. print magazine. The woman had written him a letter that stated, "Did you forget you owe me $33?" The editor had responded by sending her a check for $45.

Allegedly disinterested in the shopping activity, the man stated that he "wandered around the alley." When he returned to the shop, the man reports that a middle-aged man wearing a raincoat was just leaving. He realized that he'd left his companion's possessions, along with the shop's laptop computer, which she had borrowed, unguarded, and it had all been stolen.

The man ran into the alley in pursuit of the alleged thief, chasing him toward the street. Before the man got to his car, he threw the laptop and the woman's possessions into a sand pit. The witness was able to recover the laptop and his companion's possessions, although her electronic dictionary was broken. The undamaged laptop was returned to the owner of the boutique.

Toilet replacement error
Old toilet left in lobby

CITY — Tasked with replacing all of the school's toilets, a local man reportedly had already uninstalled several of the old ones when he realized the replacements were the wrong model, and thus the old ones had to be put back.

The recycler had allegedly already taken one of the units, and despite the fact that the man managed to catch up to him, he found that the school guard had broken the toilet's tank. The man stated that the other two uninstalled toilets were "out in the open"—one was downstairs in the lobby, and the other was upstairs next to the kindergarten.

Prairie castle besieged
"Trickery" gains access to underground farm

RURAL SASKATCHEWAN, CANADA — A visitor to the prairie province reports that he and a large group of people attempted to breach a castle wall. Other participants in the attack included his brother and sister-in-law. Afterward, the man stated that he had dirt under his thumbnail, and they stopped at a "grungy" rest stop so that he could wash it out.

The trio allegedly stayed in a cheap motel while waiting for an opportunity to tour the vast underground farm. The man reports that the three of them used trickery and a chocolate dessert recipe to fool "these buckaroo-type guys" into allowing them access to the underground farm. The farm allegedly contained plants as well as bombs, and the leader of the underground group was described as young and "articulate."

• • • • • •

Israeli desert road trip

ISRAEL — A man reported tonight that he and a high school friend were looking at maps of Northern California on his dining table. At that point they started driving around Israel, where they stayed in "someone's home" and "cooked a lot of food on a big stove."

The man states that he was wearing a dark-blue galabia, but admits that "I might have been an older woman with darker skin." The road trip reportedly went through "red, red desert" and past "blue, blue water."

At one point, the man reported that they got onto a road that was too narrow to turn the car around, and so they drove the entire circumference of a small peninsula.

• • • • • •

Fury over mangled crepes

LOCAL — A man reported a conflict with his mother after traveling to her home by car. Tasked with making crepes, the man stated that "they kept falling apart," which infuriated the woman, who allegedly struck him with a wooden spoon.

Bugs "everywhere"

LOCAL — A wide variety of bugs were "all over" a man's room, reports indicate tonight. The man stated that they were mostly wood lice, but represented many dozens of species. He allegedly stomped on some and sprayed others with bug killer, but "there were just so many."

• • • • • •

Saint spotted on ski excursion

Coworker goes mute

KANANASKIS COUNTRY, CANADA — A man visiting the region reported cross-country skiing in this foothills wilderness area with a large number of family members. The man stated that "there were lots of kids around" and that his brother told him about a new job. Also in the ski group was a work colleague who had gone mute. He communicated with the others using hand signals that had meanings like "Come to the table."

On the ski trail the man allegedly spotted a mythical being riding a wooden horse. The being was described as "larger than life" and was reportedly carrying a sword. The man stated that it was likely either Saint George or Saint Sebastian. His family members skied toward the being, and told that man that since he'd seen the entity, he should shoot into the ground near his feet. The man's brother cleaned his rifle barrel several times and inverted it "for safety."

Red wine "bad news"

CITY — A local man reported that he drank a glass of red wine tonight and "got drunk." He stated that "I knew this was bad news."

Chinese blow-dryer "powerful"

Device can't be unplugged

MAINLAND CHINA — On a visit to the Middle Kingdom, a U.S. man reported today that the blow-dryer was "extremely powerful." The man attempted to disconnect the device from the wall socket, but the wiring was allegedly "screwy," and the device

"loud and strong." Described as "like a book," the blow-dryer was reportedly part of a game in which the guards would let the man and a convict out for a few hours to play cards.

Car given as work incentive

Vehicle parked at lake

LOS ANGELES — A book editor reportedly asked a local man to work on one of his books, and as an incentive gave the man a car, described as a blue Geo Metro. The witness allegedly parked it at the lake near his parents' house, and his brother agreed to work on the vehicle. As he cleaned up around it, the man stated that there was some "deep dirt," which he just smoothed over rather than removing it.

The man reports that he formulated his response to the editor using "bright colors" and a new printer along with multiple pieces of oddly-shaped colored paper. The content of the message was allegedly "Yes, if my boss says yes, but I've got another book to work on." Reports state that a brush fire was burning nearby.

• • • • • •

Tree crew rifles cabinets

House guests help evict interlopers

LOCAL — A man reported tonight that a friend from work and her husband were guests in the home of the man's parents. Although it was well after dark, a crew was reportedly planting a large tree outside, described as "blocking the view to the east."

After his friends retired, the man was in the process of "switching off all the lights" when a blond woman from the tree-planting crew entered the house. The man confronted her but didn't ask her to leave. The woman explained that she was looking for candles to sell. Another worker, a man wearing dirty boots, entered the house, at which time the witness states that he shouted at the man to remove his boots. The worker ignored him, and he and the woman began looking through the witness's mother's cabinets.

The witness shouted at them again, and the house guests allegedly woke up. The witness stated that he threatened to call the police, and his work friend added that she had a friend on the NYPD. The interlopers then reportedly left the house. The man reported that his guests then went back to bed, even though "it was already dawn."

Garbage trucks flee west

Man escapes detection underwater

LOCAL — Sensing a looming disaster, a man reported today that many vehicles were seen fleeing westward on the highway near his family home. The man was working on a renovation project at the property, and reports that a fleet of garbage trucks was parked near the highway. The man approached the trucks, and one allegedly sprayed him with mud.

The truck did this because "I was an escaped conscript," the man explained, and stated that he hid underwater in the ditch north of the highway to escape. The trucks were later seen headed west on the highway.

Embers "uncontrollable"

Panicked theater evacuation

LOCAL — Visiting his parents' home, a man stated tonight that there were "uncontrollable" embers or sparks that occasionally broke out into flame. The man reported that the same effect was seen in large dense cities.

While watching a film in a movie house, the man alleged that the same scene of uncontrollable embers was repeated twice on the screen, causing much fright and causing the patrons to clear the theater.

The man stated that he gathered up his belongings so that he wouldn't lose them in the panicky evacuation. The man stated that "It felt like we were waiting for something to start."

. . . . . .

Springs cleaned

LOCAL — Reports tonight indicate that an area resident visited natural springs in order to clean and "bless" them. The springs were reportedly located inside a shopping mall.

The man stated that he met several elderly people who were connected with the springs, some of them allegedly with illegitimate children. The people were described as "eccentric" and "lonely."

First-date failure

Actor abandoned

LOS ANGELES — A local man reported tonight that he went on a first date with a well-known British actor, attending a crowded event. The man alleges that the actor "chastised me" for being "sucky and boring." The man then abandoned the date and had dinner with other people who were attending the event. The man stated that "I'm not completely sure, but I think I left alone."

. . . . . .

Promoting communist science

Nazi bullwhip attack unsuccessful

CITY — Tasked with promoting science for a communist country, a local man reported that "there wasn't much money budgeted for it." In the area he alleges that a Nazi with a bullwhip was attempting to strike dogs "for practice." Each time the dogs were released, however, they ran and hid around the man's bicycle, and the aggressor was unable to inflict injury.

Once he'd left the area, the man reports waiting "long and late" for a work colleague, in his car, which was parked in the man's yard, but that the colleague never came out.

Inaudible sound waves used to alter history

LOCAL — A local man alleged tonight that there exists an almost audible sound wave being used "to alter our thoughts." The message on one of the sound waves originated with the Bush family and was an attempt to convince the public to "change our idea" that the French had not actually participated in World War II, and that the Russians hadn't been our adversaries during the Cold War. The man explained that "you aren't supposed to hear it."

Uncooperative ATM

CITY — Reports today indicate that a local man attempted to use a new bank machine, described as "blue and yellow." The device allegedly refused to accept his phone.

. . . . . .

"Cartoonish" insect behavior

Toast to "Mother"

LOS ANGELES — A man reported today that he observed a neighbor talking to a June bug that was eating her grapes. Describing the scene as "like a cartoon," the man alleges that the woman was unable to catch the insect, and it subsequently turned into a butterfly. The woman's plants were subsequently moved inside mesh screens, what she described as the foundation for an organic garden for her daughter.

The man stated that he

sat at the head of the table at dinner in the garden, and made a toast to the woman, "Happy birthday, Mother," even though she wasn't his real mother, and his own mother was not present.

Fictional tax statement prepared

Multiple office supplies employed

LOCAL — A man reported tonight that he spent time preparing an elaborate fictional tax statement for a work colleague in Japan. The witness stated that he used a Sharpie and Wite-Out correction fluid, cutting and pasting parts of pages. The man conducted the work at the kitchen table in his parents' house, and alleged that one of the lightbulbs above the table was burned out.

The fictional element of the tax statement was claiming that the man had been a film distributor in Japan. After some time engrossed in the difficult task, he claims that he asked himself why he didn't just write down the truth.

· · · · · ·

Hillside car photography project

Jane Austen "unreadable"

LOS ANGELES — Reports tonight indicate that a local man drove around with a funeral director after the two had been at the gym. At night, the front desk at the gym was staffed by the man's work colleague. The man's passenger was allegedly attempting to photograph a red Jeep Cherokee that was on the road in front of them.

The funeral director al-

legedly knew the women in the Jeep, and asked them to pose with the vehicle with the taillights turned off. The man claims that they were in the hills, "heading west toward the cemetery," and thus the view was not conducive to photography because there wasn't "enough sky." The women in the Jeep allegedly took a side road that the men failed to see, and thus "we lost them."

Retiring to the funeral director's house, the man stated that he talked to his companion's mother and examined the books on her bookshelves. When he noticed a book by Jane Austen, he explained that he'd purchased the book himself, and tried to read it, but couldn't get into it. The woman found this funny, and the trio discussed humor, with the man allegedly "delivering two more one-liners."

· · · · · · ·

Mobsters murdered

Dinner party ends in bloodshed

LOS ANGELES — A local man reported that he and a friend murdered two people tonight. The men attended a dinner with two Japanese mobsters who were described as "blackmailing us." Both of the mobsters were business associates of the man's roommate, and when the roommate found out about the murders, he was reportedly "miffed."

At the dinner, the man's friend stabbed one of the mobsters in the neck; the other mobster had died earlier, but the witness alleged that "I don't know how." The two men reportedly then "got rid of the bodies." The overall experience was described as "creepy."

· · · · · · ·

Verbal assault from bicycle

Police solve case

WEST HOLLYWOOD, CALIF. — A local man reported tonight that while cycling westbound on San- ta Monica Boulevard, he yelled "Stupid" at several different cars. When he returned to his apartment, he found a police officer waiting for him. The officer informed him that "the case is solved."

The witness explained that the case in question wasn't one in which he was the troublemaker, but a case in which "I'd been burned."

Flight-time mix-up

Phone line severed by bus departure

SAN FRANCISCO — Reports tonight indicate that a man missed his return flight from a trip, as well as a subsequent flight, and was forced to make other arrangements. "I forgot that it was the next day," the man explained. He was supposed to leave at 8 a.m. on Monday after getting back on Sunday, and stated that "I realized my mistake during the afternoon on Monday."

The man allegedly attempted to call the airline on a green office phone in the kitchen, but there were three children there "playing and making noise," so

the man took the phone on the bus. The bus, however, allegedly left before the man could contact the airline for a refund. The man stated that the green phone dangled out the bus window with several yards of the cord dragging behind it on the eastbound freeway as it crossed the Bay Bridge. The man stated that he then "reeled it back in."

Local filming attracts groupies

LOS ANGELES — A local man reported that a comedian was slated to participate in the filming of a new movie in his neighborhood. Three women in the area were reportedly "dressed to the nines" in case they got the opportunity to meet the comedian.

The man states that he was tied to a tower as a

form of punishment, but even in that predicament, he was allegedly able to hurl a basketball at one of the guards.

. . . . . .

Russia-France meeting attendees sleep in canals

Canal F "key"

RURAL FRANCE — A U.S. man reported today that he had attended a Russia-France meeting at a location in the French countryside. The rural area was described as home to a series of canals that ran parallel along a gentle curve. Many of the canals were dry, no wider than the size of "small paths." The man alleges that the meeting attendees slept in the water in one of the canals on the first night.

One of the meeting attendees was reportedly angry at the event organizers the next day because of the position his child had slept in while in the water, claiming that it was "bad for his neck."

The witness states that security guards were "running around" in an attempt to keep track of Canal F, described as the "the key one." Because of the curve in the watercourses and the terrain, the guards often mixed up Canal F with Canal C. The man states that there were "about six canals in total."

Long walk to Pentagon office

WASHINGTON, D.C. — A man reported today that he has been working at the Pentagon. "I was allowed to bring a friend with me," the man explained, and stated that he had "handlers" who would walk him in to his office. The complex was described as so large that the man realized his office was much closer to a different set of streets and highways than where he'd entered. The man reported that he also considered calling a man he'd recently hooked up with who was a resident of D.C.

Emergency on Mars mission

Lengthy negotiations to seal emergency room

PLANET MARS — A man reported today that he was on the team of six that formed the first human mission to Mars, except that "I was a woman with straight red hair." Once on the planet, the man explained that "air became an issue; it was an emergency situation."

One of the team members propped open the door to the emergency room, allowing air to gradually seep out. The other team members allegedly negotiated with her, and "discussed it at length," eventually able to get safely sealed in the room. The walls were described as made of a flexible Kevlar-like material held together with Velcro.

• • • • • •

Borrowed trailer road trip

Somali couple organize reunion

IN THE COUNTRYSIDE — Today a man reported that he borrowed a long trailer and traveled the countryside with it. The trailer allegedly contained a workspace with an anvil. A Somali couple, connected to the trailer's owner, were also aboard, described as "not stowaways, but along for the ride." The man stated that he didn't meet them, but could hear them in the back of the trailer, allegedly arguing and also arranging a family reunion.

The reunion was held outside the trailer, with attendees on lawn chairs. The man explained that he wanted to leave but that he felt "guilty" doing so, abandoning the event.

• • • • • •

Escalator used to destroy tank

LOCAL — Tasked with destroying a large pressurized tank, similar to those used for propane, a man stated that he threw the tank down the escalator in "a special room" repeatedly, until the vessel burst.

Speech "involved"
Real-time translation provided

LOCAL — Reports tonight indicate that a local man was on stage "in front of a lot of people" with the husband of a former student, as the husband made a speech directed at the witness. The man reported that he read the translation of the speech in near real time from a black tablet, described as "thin like a refrigerator magnet." The speech was allegedly "an involved story."

After the speech, the man stated that he mingled with the audience members, and one woman, described as "jealous," tried to get him to leave with her.

Mountain ascent attempted
Massive redevelopment along trail

MOUNT FUJI, JAPAN — Reportedly climbing the mountain for a second time, a visitor to the island nation realized it was too late in the day, and he was unable to locate his traveling companion. After briefly meeting a college-era ex-boyfriend, the man allegedly realized that the august mountain had changed, with towns, hotels, restaurants, and other buildings lining the trail just beyond the initial "push" or first section of the mountain.

The man reported meeting a man who worked as a translator, and as they chatted, discovered that the translator had lived in his hometown. The translator was described as having "curly hair, a mustache, and was slightly femmie."

Other climbers reportedly passed the pair as they were "faster and fitter." Later, when climbing alone, the man took false turns several times, but managed to find his way from one floor of a restaurant to the next, then out onto the balcony and onward up the mountain. Eventually the man explained that he turned back before reaching the top.

. . . . . .

1940s actor to marry

Exes "cordial"

LOS ANGELES — A local man reported today that he was "hanging out" with a well-known 1940s screen actor who was getting married soon. The woman was allegedly saying goodbye to her exes, described as "happy for her."

The man drove the actor up a leafy road to the home of her fiancé, and on the way, one of her exes allegedly spotted her, and they stopped to talk. The ex was described as "cordial" and advised the actor to "cry for happiness."

Fruitless quest for inn

First female okyu leads terror attack

RURAL ENGLAND — Reports indicate that a man visiting the country with a friend spent significant time in the countryside today searching for an inn. The man stated that they were unable to find it because "the door looked like all the others in the hallway." Finally the pair abandoned the quest.

The man's traveling companion then stated that he'd just heard Kurdish terrorists had "hit a dam" in Shizuoka City, Japan. The ringleader of the attack was reported to be the first woman *okyu* in a specific sport. The two travelers, along with the woman staffing the desk at the hotel, then attempted to figure out the meaning of *okyu*.

[*Editor's note:* at press time, the meaning of *okyu* had not been determined. Similar words in Japanese indicate moxibustion, emergency response (応急), a processed fish product (おきゅうと), a royal palace (王宮), and even pain-relief dermal patches (おきゅ膏). This story will be updated as new details become available.]

• • • • • • •

Slow retail; auxiliary apartment unused

TOKAI REGION, JAPAN — A resident of the area reported working in a store that was described as "very quiet." After work, the man allegedly accompanied his roommate to their second apartment. The man stated that he wanted to check for water damage. The building's owner was in the unit, renovating it. The man stated that "it was supposed to be our studio, but we never used it."

Airport tigers "causing trouble"

LAX — A man reported today that the free-range tigers residing at the airport were "causing trouble for me." The guards at the airport allegedly then agreed to x-ray one of the creatures.

Humorous video with giant bird, dynamite

Family members enlisted in production

LOCAL — A man reported that a friend of his mother's was directing a music video today at a nearby pond. The video was described as "humorous" and "like a cartoon" in which three children walking through marshy underbrush get shot. Two of the man's siblings were reportedly engaged to operate "the weird big puppet bird" for the shoot. As the director filmed the scene, another of the man's siblings was in the water, setting off dynamite to simulate gunfire. With each explosion, the large bird puppet reportedly threw up a handful of feathers to simulate being struck by gunfire.

The man stated that the production "came off perfectly" and "it was really funny." He explained that the video also included a "toast scene" that was based on work with real birds and toasts.

Parents donate TV set

"Keep him on loser"

LOCAL — While visiting the home of his parents, a man reported that they offered him their old oversize television set because they were upgrading their own. The man alleged that the pair put on their headphones and then adjusted the device's control dials.

The man's mother then said, "Keep him on 'loser,'" meaning the noise filter.

The man reported that he found the series of events humorous, and sought out his siblings to tell them about it.

. . . . . .

Windows '97 rip-off

CITY — A local man reported that he received a special application for Windows '97 software, but alleges that "It's a rip-off because it only puts a photo up on the screen. That's all it does."

Editor oversells minor revision

LOS ANGELES — A local office worker revealed today that the chief editor of the magazine came to his desk today to work through a revision to a page about job surveys. "This really has to make you feel like you'll get your job back," the editor explained, among many other comments, and also allegedly cracked a joke about the man going hiking so often. The man stated that the revision was "really minuscule, just adding a single credit to the byline."

Restroom gender debate

Huge "walk-in" sinks

LOCAL — Concerns were reported tonight about gays and straights using the same restrooms. Eventually it was decided that restrooms would be segregated into male and female, rather than gay and straight. A local man reportedly aided in rearranging the cubicles in the newly segregated restrooms, under the supervision of what he described as "the matriarch."

The sinks in the man's apartment were reportedly "huge" and designed to be walk-in, with a hinged gate "like at an ice rink."

Bugs still in food

LOCAL — Dining with his sister and brother, a local man reported that someone had neglected to remove the bugs from the potatoes and other vegetables. Described as green and less than ¼ inch wide and ½ to 1 inch long, the man allegedly picked them out of the food as the trio chatted.

Scarves produced at twelve-step meeting

Gas fireplace confusion

LOS ANGELES — Attending a twelve-step meeting tonight, a local man reported that among those present was a teacher-counselor, and that the president of the group was a friend from grade school. The president asked the man to light the fireplace, and the man reportedly proceeded to first disconnect the gas line. Another meeting attendee allegedly "started to freak out" when the witness asked him how to turn off the fireplace, believing that the procedure was more dangerous than it actually was.

The other attendee then took over the task, and went inside the fire room for the duration of the meeting. He produced some silk scarves that were described as "beautiful" and with metal decorations, including some designs that were based on tarot cards.

. . . .

Host, son both wheelchair users
Garden "thin," "weak"

LOCAL — Reports tonight indicate that a man visited the home of an acquaintance who used a motorized wheelchair. Both the host and his son used motorized wheelchairs, and the witness stated that they parked them "carefully" at the dining table. When the son retrieved a mug from the cupboard, the man reportedly said that the cupboard was "crowded, like at my place."

The older man discussed the garden, and made a joke about how thin and weak the soil was. "You could take out a plug," the man allegedly stated, "and replace it with an ice cream cone, and in a few months you could still see through it all."

. . . .

Police arrest former tenant's roommate
Drug crimes alleged

WEST HOLLYWOOD, CALIF. — A man reports today that he has been living in the former apartment of a work colleague on Harper Avenue. From outside the man reportedly heard a young man shouting the woman's name. The man reportedly then began to write down the woman's new address for him, but then witnessed the police chase the man on foot and detain him.

When the police officers visited the apartment, the man allegedly told them that the woman's former roommate had been a drug dealer. The officers informed him that the woman was also a dealer, to his great surprise. The man reported that "I can't believe I wouldn't have known that."

The man stated that the officers then "hung out" for some time, sitting around the apartment with him and a woman friend.

"Large quantity" of waffles consumed

Factory workers enlisted in food prep

LOCAL — Reports tonight indicate that a man consumed a large quantity of waffles. Cooking the waffles were workers from a Japanese factory, described as wearing uniforms that were color-coded by job class. The man stated that he and a sibling and a roommate shared several boxes of the waffles, eating them directly out of the wok. The wok itself was described as "like

a diorama of Washington, D.C.," and inside, the waffles contained tofu.

· · · · · ·

Pre-dinner religious discussion

B-list actors "unknown"

LOCAL — Reports tonight indicate that the mother of a local resident hosted a dinner party that allegedly featured several Los Angeles B-list celebrities as guests, as well as two celebrities from the Quebec film industry. "I only knew who one of them was," the man stated.

Before the meal, the

guests "sat around chatting," and the man stated that one of his mother's former work colleagues arrived, and the two women discussed the woman's daughter.

Several of the guests pointed out the crucifix that the man was wearing. He allegedly explained that he hadn't realized it was a religious symbol, and wore it to attach his keys to when he went jogging. The man then offered the crucifix to anyone who wanted it.

The man's father then stated humorously that "There's something to be said for taking your parents' religion," to which the man reportedly concurred. One of his siblings then talked about taking on parts of some Eastern religions.

Missing cash found

Counting interrupted by interlopers

LOCAL — An area resident reported today that he couldn't find "the wad of yen" that he'd hidden at his parents' house "when all of our stuff got moved." Outside in the yard, next to the well, the man saw a stack of books, and went out to go through them. He alleged that the Japanese cash was discovered here, in a bag, and totaled about ¥90,000. The man stated that he counted it on the sofa, arranging the bills in piles by denomination, but "felt wary" when other people came around, including a former student accompanied by her friend as well as the man's brother.

· · · · · ·

Frenchman berates workers

Outdoor chef burns paper

CITY — A man reported tonight that he sat on a divan and watched a Frenchman across the street berate two workers. The man stated that "one of the workers was dark-skinned, and the other was light-skinned." The pair were directed to stand at attention while the Frenchman spoke. The man stated that the situation was humorous, and both workers were described as "hot."

The witness then walked down the street, allegedly into a different area code, where a chef was cooking outdoors. The chef reportedly burned some colored paper, red and purple, which the man stated "looked cool." As the chef turned his wrist to check his watch, he allegedly inadvertently thrust his chef's knife toward the witness's face.

· · · · · ·

Dioramas fully cover floor
Resentments build over clearances

LOCAL — Reports tonight indicate that a man and his brother built dioramas of the city that covered the entire floor. Each family member allegedly had a section of the floor. The man stated that his was dense with city high-rises, while his brother's contained curving streets, and another area was mostly strewn feathers.

The man's mother and another sibling cleared away part of the dioramas, in the lake region, so that they could sit down. Upset with their actions, the man allegedly confronted them, but his mother ignored him at first. The man stated that he carried resentment about the matter for some time.

· · · · · ·

Virtual parking lot shit requires new "keys"
Alien jokes about parking spaces

LOS ANGELES — Reports tonight indicate that persons unknown have been leaving shit outside the restrooms in the shared beach parking lot co-owned by a local man. The man explained that the shit was digital, not physical. In discussions with another of the parking lot owners, the decision was made to address the problem by getting all 4.5 of the users new keys, which were, in reality, passwords. Though reportedly difficult, the plan would either eliminate the problem or limit it to one of the four full users.

The fractional user, a Hollywood actor, invited the man to her home, where he found that another guest was a gray alien. The man states that he joked with the alien that the actor had agreed to help with the parking lot investigation by not parking in the best spots near the exit. The witness stated that he and the alien "laughed and rolled around on the bed."

Homeless man burns shoe, asks for cash

LOS ANGELES — In a local park today a man reports that he was walking around with a female friend. A homeless man in the park allegedly lit his shoe on fire, then put it out, and subsequently approached the pair and asked for forty cents. When the man refused to pay, the homeless man allegedly leaned very close to him. "I put my hand on his chest and pushed him back to arm's length," the man explained. "I told him to keep a social distance."

Dirty hands before dinner

Plan to sit next to crush

LOCAL — Reports tonight indicate that a local man attended a dinner party with a large number of guests, including his parents and a man that he stated that he was "hot for." Before the meal, the attendees were reportedly sitting around talking, and the man stated that he was petting a cat. Inadvertently scratching a cyst under the cat's neck, the man got the animal's pus on his hand. The man rose and announced to the other guests that "I'm going to wash off the cat ... hair." The man's father allegedly admonished him for the remark.

When he was at the sink washing his hands, the host called the guests to dinner. The man stated that he intended to sit next to the man he was interested in, so that "I could touch him."

Eyeglasses shattered in night encounter

Youths assist in recovery

THE COUNTRYSIDE — A visitor to the area tonight reported walking up a dark mountain road. On the left he observed a group of "shadowy figures" standing and looking out over a valley. "I figured they were *yankīs*," the man explained. [*Editor's note:* In Japan *yankī* (ヤンキー) is a type of delinquent youth culture whose participants wear pompadours, punch perms, and artificially blond hair, and are sometimes associated with underworld organizations.]

The man attempted to walk around the group, on the right side, but because of the darkness, "I bumped

into one of them." The group assisted the man to sit down on the edge of the road, where he allegedly discovered that his glasses had been shattered. "I could then see better," the man admitted, and the group examined him and his glasses for injuries. The man's next-door neighbor soon arrived and also examined the glasses.

· · · · · ·

Reality TV group a panoply of former classmates

TOKAI REGION, JAPAN — Returning to the island nation after a lengthy absence, a Los Angeles man reported tonight that a group of people down the street were participating in a twenty-four-hour live reality show on television. When he went to visit the group, the man discovered that one of the participants was a classmate he had last seen in second grade. The classmate allegedly borrowed some Vicodin "for a migraine." Another classmate, from middle school, was also one of the participants, but the man stated that "he avoided me." A friend from college was part of the group as well, and the man stated that he hugged the friend and invited him to LA.

As the man was leaving the reality TV group, he took his shirt off, and a woman he'd last seen in high school allegedly called him "fat." The man stated that he reacted by "making a joke of it" and that he "acted coquettish."

• • • • • •

Lengthy trek to restrooms

Witness waffles on own identity

VAIL, COLO. — A winter visitor to the ski resort reported tonight that he was staying in a dorm room with what he described as "an American guy." The pair left their beds in search of a restroom, a quest that saw them walk through a "huge crowded lobby," down a flight of stairs, and through a busy nightclub. The woman staffing the door of the nightclub allegedly made a joke about "keeping your hands off your dick" while inside the club.

The pair eventually located the restroom, described as "massive" with the urinals on an upper floor and the toilet cubicles downstairs. Inside, the man reports that he ran into a couple of classmates from high school. The men explained that they had entered the restroom through the corridor rather than via the nightclub.

When he was inside one of the cubicles, one of his high school peers allegedly looked over the top of the cubicle wall and asked the man to confirm his identity, but the man stated that he waffled. The interloper reportedly said, "The cubicle door is locked," implying that it was safe to respond. The witness states that he finally said, "That's not me." The witness explained that "I'm content with who I am, but I didn't want a reunion."

Funds smuggled out of the country

Overseas trip in a '74 Plymouth

CITY — A local man reported tonight that he volunteered to help an old friend who had recently "come into some money" to transport the funds out of the country. The man claimed that they had to maneuver carefully, as many people knew about the money, and they didn't want to get robbed.

While the pair were making preparations to leave the country, a "9/11-style disaster" allegedly occurred. Among those present were a cinematic actor, a family of Germans distantly related to the man by marriage, and two mechanics. The mechanics were reportedly tasked with working on the man's 1974 Plymouth so that it would be ready for the pair to drive it to Japan. "We were being so careful with everyone," the man explained, "because we didn't want to give away where the money was hidden."

· · · · · ·

Mismatched jousting weaponry

Sex, death feature in battle

LOCAL — A man reported today that he got into a jousting match with two opponents. The man stated that he was armed with a sword and a whip but no horse, while both opponents had horses and jousting poles. Despite the mismatched weaponry, the man alleged that he managed to fend off his opponents' attacks.

One of the opponents then allied with the man, and together they managed to beat the third man to the ground. The man's new ally reportedly cut his hand twice, and when the man approached, he allegedly slit his ally's throat.

Describing the incident as "horrible," the man stated that he then "undid" the violent act and "unkilled" his ally, described as a blond with a light beard. The two then proceeded to have sex.

Book business busted

LOCAL — A man reported today that his brother, while visiting his office, was reading a book from the man's desk. He allegedly asked his brother whether the book was interesting, to which he replied, "I'll give it back to you when I'm finished with it, so you can sell it." Other workers in the office overheard the exchange, and the man's side business of surreptitiously selling off the company's books was revealed.

LDS couple win honeymoon contest

LOS ANGELES — A local man reported tonight that he was running a contest for honeymooners to win a night in a hotel. A Latter-day Saint couple reportedly won the contest. In consultation with an LDS youth and a local woman, the man learned that the couple would be undertaking elaborate wedding-night rituals. Despite these complications, the man stated that he decided just to welcome them in the usual way.

· · · · · ·

Man blanks on guests' names

LOS ANGELES — Reports tonight indicate that a man has been hosting a family of six, including several children, at his home. He stated that he planned events for the visitors that included a day at the public swimming pool. He introduced the family to a classmate from high school, who was also visiting, but stated that during the introduction he blanked out on everyone's names. His high school friend was described as having a pinched face and black bowl-cut hair, and "had grown short and fat."

Boat passengers "cool," "focused"

VANCOUVER, CANADA — A local folk singer asked a man to descend a rocky hillside toward the beach. Several people were there in a motorized inflatable boat, and the folk singer introduced the man to the group. The pair climbed into the boat, which subsequently traveled out onto the water.

Besides the witness and the folk singer, the other passengers were described as her boyfriend, in his forties; a young woman with dark hair; and a young man with stubble and a hairstyle described as "mod." The witness claimed that the group exuded "coolness" and seemed energized and focused on the task at hand rather than "playing games."

• • • • • •

Land converted for free-range cattle

Cups, towels packed

OUT WEST — A man reported today that the entirety of his parents land had been converted into free-range land for cattle. A blue sign served as a symbolic gate to the land, and a cattle grid acted as a more tangible gate. The man states that he attempted to convince his brother and father that they should sell the cattle as organic, explaining that organic cows had a nutritional advantage.

Later, the witness reportedly worked in the house packing boxes of cups and towels for shipment to his parents. The man stated that he had to remove some of his camping equipment from boxes to obtain enough empty boxes for his parents' cup racks.

• • • • • •

No injuries in light aircraft crash
Incident witnessed from kitchen window

IN THE COUNTRYSIDE — while standing at the kitchen window of his parents' home, a man visiting the area today reported that he witnessed a red Cessna aircraft stall out and plummet to the ground. The man stated that he alert-ed his father and others. When they went outdoors to check on the crash, the pilot allegedly climbed out of the wreck unharmed. The pilot and his passenger turned out to be his parents' neighbors.

• • • • • •

Hand puppet a mathematical plane
Closed-sphere conceptualization erroneous

LOCAL — A man reported tonight that he discovered that a hand puppet is actually a mathematical plane, rather than a closed sphere. This story will be updated as further details warrant.

Kitchen subsiding
Noodle, flax, mayonnaise dish served

LOCAL — Reportedly invited for a visit to his parents' home, a man reported today that there was a special kettle provided there for his exclusive use to boil water. The kitchen of the house was described as subsiding. The man's brother allegedly promised to repair the subsidence.

On the drive to his parents home, the man reported that a complex of buildings was under construction near the highway, with lots of cars parked around, and a couple of large Haida sculptures perched at the top of the cliffs. The man and his brother speculated that it might be a hotel. The highway was described as "very potholed" and "a bit worrying" in the snow.

At his parents' home,

the man's father allegedly cooked him egg noodles served with flaxseed and a dollop of mayonnaise. His father reportedly provided a cooking fork to eat the meal with.

. . . . . .

Dragons instruct on mental states

LOS ANGELES — A man reported tonight that some dragons had specific instructions for him and his roommates in order to achieve a specific mental state. The witness was allegedly unsure whether the state of mind was "in the dragons' best interests, or in ours." The instructions reportedly involved "becoming something at a different time."

Range legs adjusted

Connection to playground equipment

LOCAL — Reports tonight indicate that a man helped his mother raise the front legs of her kitchen range. The man stated that it was his idea, as the stove was leaning outward. Several small children helped in the work.

The witness's brother and sister arrived "at the last minute" and adjusted the playground equipment at the back of the house that was all connected to the range. The witness stated that he was annoyed at first, but that his siblings insisted that "it's all connected." The range was said to be located outside, near the road by the school.

. . . . . .

Floor cleaning interrupted

Dog sniffs butt "for too long"

LOCAL — An area resident stated that while cleaning the house, he was sweeping the hardwood floor because there were allegedly "mountains of cat litter" around and under the carpet. He stated that he moved bales of fabric from around the sofa.

The man's niece then reportedly dropped by

with an unknown boyfriend. The woman's dog, described as a skinny greyhound, then thrust its nose "right up near my butt for way too long." The man reportedly swatted the dog with a broom and told him, "Stop sniffing my ass." The man stated that he was embarrassed because there were people in another part of the room.

· · · · · ·

Devil seen in local garage

Offended by lumber mishap

SUBURBIA — The devil was reportedly "hanging out" in a local man's father's garage tonight, and the man claimed that he was "afraid" of the prince of darkness. The devil was described as shaved-headed and wearing jeans, a coat, and a woolen cap. Also present was one of the man's former students, whom the witness alleges was "either his disciple or under his influence."

The man claims that he accidentally dumped a pile of lumber on the devil. After the man's student freed him from the lumber, the devil decided to kill the man in retaliation, using a single rifle shell. The man allegedly asked the devil for a few minutes' reprieve in order to pray "so that I could get into heaven." The subsequent rapid sequence of events has not been clearly elucidated, but the man reported that he managed to take a shotgun off the garage's wall rack and "blew the devil away." This story will be updated as further details become available.

· · · · · ·

Chance meeting with potter

LOS ANGELES — Reports today indicate that a local man ran into an old acquaintance, a potter from Denmark, accompanied by several of her friends. The chance meeting with the women happened on a city street while the man was cycling. He and the potter allegedly exchanged a long hug, and spent a

few minutes catching up, but the man stated that he "forgot" to get her phone number or any other details that would allow him to contact her again.

Bathrooms locked

Unknown models "waiting"

LOS ANGELES — On waking tonight, a local man reports that he found the door to his bathroom closed and locked. He could hear the voice of his roommate inside talking to another person. The roommate's bathroom was also allegedly closed and locked.

In the living room of the apartment, the man allegedly found two clothing models seated on the sofa "waiting." Strewn on a newly assembled table near the front door were several clothing patterns. The witness stated that there was also a smudge from a grubby hand on his bathroom door. He reported that he thought at first that someone might be doing repairs.

Invisible fleas "annoying"

LOCAL — Reportedly waking up tonight to unpleasant itching, a local man stated that he had some kind of fleas or bugs on his neck, and that they were "really annoying." The man stated that he asked his mother for assistance. She was reportedly still awake, even though it was very late, but she was unable to assist him because she was going out for an undisclosed reason. The man's brother was also awake, and he asked him for help. The fleas or insects were described as "invisible."

Stare-down for café table

TV broadcast "funny"

SAN FRANCISCO — Seated at a café table today, a man reported that his former neighbor and a friend wanted the table when the man left. Allegedly in no hurry to leave, the man explained that he was writing something with a broken pen. The café manager reportedly told the two men to "move along," but they stood nearby and stared at the witness, allegedly attempting to intimidate him.

The television in the café was reportedly showing an episode of *The Beverly Hillbillies* in which Ellie Mae was attending a second debutante ball, after the one she participated in when she was poor. The episode was described as "funny."

Cash taken from briefcase

"Russian mafia" ruse to secure return

LOCAL — After visiting his sister at a large shopping mall, a local man reported that the woman walked him out to his truck. A Russian man who had borrowed the vehicle had allegedly taken two bundles of cash from the witness's briefcase that had been left in the truck. The witness stated that he drove around with the alleged thief, and in an effort to scare him into returning the funds, told him "false tales" that the Russian mafia were the actual owners of the cash.

· · · · · ·

Passengers forced to clean lavatory

Gloves, toilet brush provided

LOCAL — A man reported today that he traveled first-class on a 707 aircraft along with some businessmen. Because it was before planes were "sophisticated," each passenger who used the lavatory was required to take the bright-yellow transparent rubber gloves and toilet brush from their little complimentary toiletries kit for use in the lavatory. Reports indicate that the lavatory smelled like cleanser.

The witness stated that on board the aircraft, he examined the stationary kits in the seat pocket, but both of the kits had been written on. They were described as "a pretty blue-green" with airplane logos. The man alleged that a woman was hogging the lavatory in the last part of the flight before landing.

· · · · · ·

Rude behavior leads to argument

LOS ANGELES — When he reportedly refused to order a drink and told the server to "have an awful day," a local man stated that his roommate, seated with him at the outdoor café, "freaked out" and argued with him about his behavior. The man allegedly then left the café.

· · · · · ·

Aspirins melted on tongue for TV

Features not pleasing

LOS ANGELES — Looking into a mirror, a man reported tonight that he placed aspirins on his tongue and watched them melt. The purpose of the activity was allegedly that the man was being filmed for a television commercial. The man further stated that his features, as seen in the mirror, were "exaggerated" and "I didn't like

the look of them."

· · · · · ·

Poor tour planning alleged

Too much walking

OTTAWA, CANADA — A man and his roommate and a mutual friend allegedly organized a tour to the Canadian capital today for a pair of students. The man claims that he didn't know where the group was staying and became separated from them. Although he managed to meet up with them again, the witness stated that the tour was "misplanned," with lots of walking.

One of the tour organizers worked to convince the witness to drink beer, "just one sip," thus breaking his sobriety, but then another person talked him out of doing so. Subsequently walking to the city's canal on his own, the witness alleged that there were "huge waves" on the water. The man sought a bridge over the canal to go west, and described rain showers. He stated that his return walk was "much like the Tōkaidō Line." [*Editor's note:* The Tōkaidō (東海道) line is the main passenger rail line along the Pacific coast between Tokyo and Kobe, Japan.]

· · · · · ·

Old West mass murder site found

Plaster models indicate details

OUT WEST — Reports tonight indicate that the site of an Old West mass murder has been found. A visitor to the gold mining camp reported being guided through how each death had occurred, illustrated with plaster models that indicated the locations of the bodies and other details.

Bees give chase

LOS ANGELES — Reports today indicate that a local man inadvertently irritated some bees, which then swarmed and chased after him. The man admitted that he received a few stings. Someone advised the man to turn away from the bees into the wind, and he stated that "that seemed to help."

New employee "messes up"

Reprimand "serious"

LOS ANGELES — An area resident reported today that he was able to obtain employment for a friend from Australia at his company. The friend reportedly "messed up" in the new job by neglecting to put a label on a file folder. The new employee's supervisor reprimanded him in front of other staffers, and in response he defended his nomadic lifestyle. The discussion reportedly went back and forth, "serious but not angry." The witness believed that neither one of them was backing down because both were afraid of losing face in front of him.

Ambitious diving trip

THE GREEK ISLANDS — A U.S. visitor to the area reported tonight that he took a scuba-diving excursion with his brother. The pair planned to dive along the full length of a local bay to enjoy the classical atmosphere.

· · · · · ·

Makeshift yarmulke employed

Street crossing elicits "grumbling"

LOS ANGELES — A city resident reported today that he crossed the street with a large group of Hasidic Jewish men. The man stated that he put a dollar bill on his head in place of a yarmulke, and subsequently several foreign tourists did the same thing. The Hasidim reportedly reacted by "grumbling."

The man's boyfriend, described as "actually Jewish," decided then that they should not attend the event. The witness stated that he had the realization in that moment that his boyfriend was actually open-minded for getting involved with him. The boyfriend allegedly stated that he was going to require the movers to wear yarmulkes when they moved their belongings from the bar to their new residence.

· · · · · ·

Croatia road trip

Road maps gradually deciphered

CROATIA — Reports today indicate that a U.S. man rode around postwar Croatia in a car with "a couple of guy friends." The group allegedly had paper maps of Croatia's cities that they were deciphering electronically. The man described himself as the "map pro" for the trip. Slowly figuring out what was what, the group drove into the heart of a historic fortress and were able to locate a gas station on a rural road.

Serious argument leads to broken "stuff"

Drinking with Norman

LOS ANGELES — Reports tonight indicate that a local man got into a "breakdown" verbal altercation with a friend. The woman had reportedly told the man that she had been drinking with someone named Norman, and told the man to "shut up." In response he allegedly "broke some stuff."

Course filmed for TV

Handstand stunt "to find bride"

LOCAL — A man reported tonight that he participated in an athletics and driver's ed course that was filmed for television. The principal organizer was reported to be the man's father. Another man, described as "a chunky Russian," taught the course. The witness alleges that the teacher wanted to do a handstand flip stunt for the cameras in order to find himself a bride.

· · · · · ·

Dam break causes flood

Ex's status unknown

TOKAI REGION, JAPAN — Reports tonight indicate that heavy rains and a simultaneous earthquake caused a dam to fail on the Warashina River. An area resident stated that he saw the dam fail, but that the friend he was with "was in denial about it, talking about other stuff." The man reportedly confronted her about "not feeling anything" when he was concerned that some of his friends could have been killed.

The witness stated that he grew concerned about an ex-boyfriend whose home was downstream, next to the river. He allegedly then traveled to the home of other friends, and hugged them when he found them unharmed. The entire flood plain had reportedly turned green, and the man stated that he planned to walk along the tram tracks to his ex's house, hopeful that the tram was still running, or at least that the tracks were accessible.

· · · · · ·

Space shuttle in low flyby

Vehicle smoking, drops equipment

LOS ANGELES — While waiting aboard a bus at a local airfield, a man claimed that a fellow passenger recognized him as a hostage in a maritime hijacking incident several years ago. The individual claimed to be an acquaintance of a child who was also held hostage in the incident. "She was one of the cutest kids on the ship," the man explained. "My memory of her is that she looked like a little duck, and wore a green plaid hat and suit."

During the interlude aboard the bus, the space shuttle flew over the airfield at extremely

low altitude. "It had its doors open," the witness claimed, "and it was flying low, closer and closer to the ground, with awful diesel smoke coming out the back." Other passengers reportedly expressed concern that the shuttle was going to crash, but as they watched, it didn't. "It just dropped off this flatbed trailer with lots of wheels," the witness explained. "The shuttle then lifted up again, without a problem, and looped around." The flatbed trailer had been dropped facing the other way, the witness reported, "but it came whizzing by our bus. It was all dusty."

"Happier" with brain enhancer

IN THE WOODS — A group of high school students reportedly took a brain enhancer while on a camping trip "as an experiment." The students reported feeling "better" and "happier." The group's leader shredded her blouse in a fashionable way, then apologized to the teacher accompanying the group.

Australian tour planned

Rednecks demand inflated final rent payment

LOCAL — Staying with a group of what he described as "chubby rednecks," an area resident reported that he was preparing to move out and undertake a tour of Australia with a school group. The man admitted that his plan was to ditch the tour group and stay with a friend in Melbourne, because "I've done the touring thing enough."

As he was preparing to take a shower, one of the rednecks, a woman, allegedly told the man to prepare his final rent check. Described as "obese," the woman reportedly wore thick-lensed eyeglasses as well as fuchsia and purple hair in "a big swirl" covering most of her face.

The woman told him that the rent due was $660, but the man stated that the usual amount was $330, and there was no reason for him to pay for two months. The woman and her husband explained that the rent was for the new residence, not for the previous residence, where the rent had been $330. The man reportedly said, "That's the first I've heard of it," and explained that he would check with the school administrators, and if they agreed, he would pay the additional amount. The man stated that he was proud of himself for standing up to them, and admitted that even at the time he was well aware that even the initial $330 check was "rubber."

Train passengers disembark to "play"

Witness well-known on board

IN THE MOUNTAINS — Reportedly alone in a clearing in the mountains, a man stated that he picked up a piece of dusty yellow fabric. A train came through the clearing and stopped, allowing some Australian children to disembark and play. The children reportedly knew the man's name, and he told them, "That surprises me." The children explained that several people aboard the train knew who he was. The man then allegedly remembered that his brother had told him something similar, that he'd been aboard a train where several passengers knew the witness's name.

· · · · · · ·

Careful smoking avoids addiction

CITY — A local man reported sitting on a half flight of outdoor concrete stairs tonight and experimenting with smoking. He described taking "small puffs and big puffs" and stated that if he smoked carefully, he wouldn't get addicted.

Tar Heel cuisine "bland"

Worms and larvae spread from container

LOS ANGELES — Attending a meeting described as a think-tank event, a local man stated that food from different regions was served. The dish from North Carolina was reportedly dark larvae with black worms among them. Told that they were indeed food, the man tried them, but stated that they were bland. Later he allegedly walked around talking to other meeting attendees and "kept finding the worms on him," reportedly because the canvas lid of the container didn't fit properly. The worms were also seen on the floor. The man stated that he thought he knew who had brought the problematic dish.

Reported for work in wrong city

Old purse discovered

SAN FRANCISCO — A Los Angeles man reportedly arrived at his company's San Francisco office today to start the new work year. Riding the subway to the office, he alleged that he spoke to a man that he found attractive, and asked him about a shop, but the man didn't know the place.

On arriving at his company's building, the man reportedly realized that he was supposed to be in Los Angeles, not here. His boss then reportedly showed

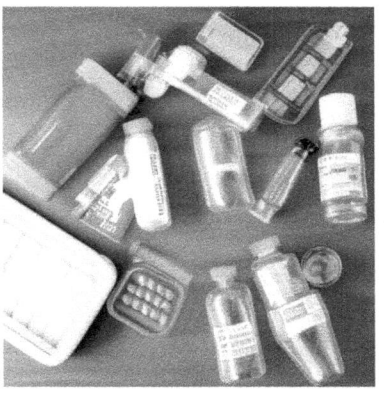

up "to straighten me out." The woman allegedly discovered an old purse in the lobby that contained some of her medications.

· · · · · ·

Siblings wait in lobby

People dressed for winter

LOS ANGELES — A man reported tonight that his brother was avoiding contact with his mother because she had prepared a kind of salmon that he didn't like but that he "couldn't admit it." The man allegedly asked him what the secret was, and when his brother told him, he stated that he "blew the whistle."

Later the man's brother and another sibling were reportedly waiting for him in the lobby of his apartment building in the Miracle Mile district. The man found a parking spot a block east, in a zone signed as "15 minutes parking Wednesday for recycling." The man allegedly left his car there because it was Tuesday and jogged back to his building to meet his siblings.

On entering the building's lobby, his brother reportedly greeted him with a long string of fake names. Also waiting on the lobby furniture was a straight couple. As the man and his siblings left, other people were going in, including a woman who spoke with an accent when asking directions to a business in the building. The witness asked her what she was looking for, but someone else, a young woman wearing a wooly cap, was already giving her directions. The man stated that the people in the lobby were dressed for early winter, with pink being the dominant color of their clothing.

Texas local flavor explored

TEXAS — A man visiting from out of state reported staying with local people and seeing some "idiosyncratic local stuff," allegedly including a chicken dance as well as a roadway rail crossing on a curve that was described as "very dangerous."

Low turnout for reunion

Outfits "similar"

LOCAL — Reports tonight indicate that a high school reunion event was attended by just three former students. A local man stated that he was joined by a woman and a man from his class. The other man was allegedly dressed almost the same as he was,

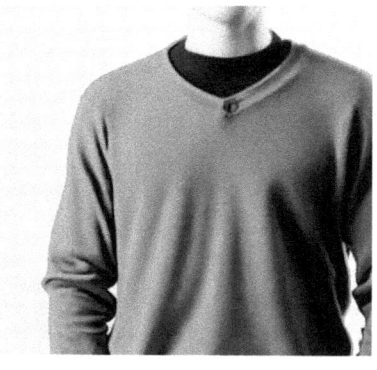

in a black shirt, red sweater, and jeans, although the other man's sweater was a vest, and the witness stated that his own had sleeves. The woman attendee then allegedly pinched the other man's buttocks "for some reason"; the witness reported feeling embarrassed for her.

· · · · · ·

Return to the '80s

CITY — A man reported tonight that he and a group of other people were able to travel back to the 1980s. The man stated that "Margaret Thatcher was there" and that a complex formula existed to determine when they were, then or now.

Church service skipped for shopping

Bookstore sells tea, hardware

COTSWOLDS, UK — A man reported that his sister-in-law reserved a pew for several family members for a special service in a small Church of England outpost in the region. The man reportedly arrived first, and used the restroom in the church, then went to a nearby bookstore. He allegedly ran into a friend in the shop, and exchanged an awkward hug. The man suggested that she ask which pew was reserved for their use.

Browsing the store, the man allegedly discovered a huge green tea section, and a section dedicated to hardware. Reportedly "distracted by porn," including Japanese anime erotica, in the store, the man almost shoplifted a book, but then remembered to pay for it when the clerk, described as an old man, asked another customer for a receipt.

Exiting the store, the man reportedly realized that he'd missed the entire church service. At home, he attempted to explain to his roommates what had happened, but one of them interrupted him, saying, "If you didn't want to go, you didn't want to go, that's it." Because the woman allegedly didn't let him talk, when she said something a minute later, he responded with "Fuck you." When she attempted to speak again, he allegedly said, "If I'm not allowed to talk, neither are you. Fuck you."

Cooking class confusion
Cilantro, olive oil employed

ON CAMPUS — Today a local man reported that he was late for his university cooking class because "I had to get the mail." There was allegedly so much mail that he dropped several pieces of it as he arrived at the class. The professor then asked the man to start a dish based on cilantro and olive oil. Once the witness had done the prep work, the prof took over the cooking process, and the man was asked to go to the supermarket at the back of campus to purchase cilantro.

The man proceeded to prepare a dish that was described as "dough-like" and "sweet and sticky." After the class members had filled their plates, the man's mother stated that she couldn't stay. The man then allegedly asked another student, described as "a goofy guy," to eat with him. The other student had planned to retire to his car to read the newspaper, but after the witness asked a second time, he agreed to eat with him.

Leisure time in Parliament building
Drainpipe provides potable water

OTTAWA, CANADA — A man visiting Parliament, the seat of Canada's government, reported that he spent time today "playing on the banisters." After seeing a former Minister of International Trade crossing the lawn outside, the man reportedly "made a drainpipe work" so that he and a colleague could drink from it. The water reportedly ran clear after a few minutes of producing muddy water. The man stated that "I might have sucked on it too much, because it started blowing air."

Multiple missile launches spotted

Media silent

LOCAL — A man reported tonight that he witnessed a series of missile launches in the west, "over by the highway." Six or eight columns of flame were allegedly seen ascending into the sky through the mist. The man stated that "we expected the worst" but there was no report of the launches on the television news.

The man stated that he couldn't get the television set to change away from the children's channels, so his father assisted him, but there was still no reporting about missile launches. After some discussion, the pair theorized that it must have been a test or an exercise.

Rushed prep for spaceflight

Jeans chosen over chinos

LOS ANGELES — A local man and his roommates were reportedly invited to fly on the space shuttle tonight. The man stated that he arrived home late, to find his roommates and several work colleagues waiting for him and "ready to go." The man reportedly took a shower, and because he was "in a rush," rolled his shit into doughy balls, described as spotted brown and white, with the texture of cookie dough.

The man then proceeded to ask one of his colleagues whether he should wear chinos or jeans for the spaceflight, to which the man allegedly answered derisively, "jeans." Not taking the time to pack, the man just took a toothbrush and went outside to join the group waiting impatiently for him. His preparations had taken just twenty minutes: it was reportedly 25 after, and he'd arrived home at 5 after.

· · · · · ·

Coming out reduces tensions
Trucks try to "make time"

LOCAL — Tension was reportedly brewing today between a trucking company executive and his two assistants. The source of the tension allegedly included, in part, that the assistants assumed the exec was straight. When the man subsequently came out during a television interview, the situation was said to improve.

A local man reported that he was cycling on a local highway where the company's trucks were "trying to make time."

Sexual overtures alleged
Cupboard ideal for trash can

CITY — While showing a friend his new apartment, a local man explained that several women had allegedly made sexual overtures since he'd moved in, including a blond described as "brassy" as well as a "mousy" brunette. The man reportedly then noticed a cupboard in the kitchen, below the counter to the right of the range, that he stated would be "perfect" for a trash can, as it sloped down slightly.

Apartment "yang"
Hospital table in bedroom

LOS ANGELES — Reports tonight indicate that a local man attended a party at the apartment of one of his coworkers along with other members of the office staff. The apartment was allegedly decorated in dark reds and wood tones. The man stated that he commented to his host how yang the apartment was compared to his yin office at work.

The man alleged that when he had the opportu- nity to surreptitiously look into the bedroom, there was a hospital table set up beside the bed.

Lengthy delays in pool admission

Aztec-pattern towel involved

LOCAL — Reports today indicate that an area resident waited an inordinate amount of time to get into a local swimming pool. Although he was the only one waiting at first, the lone staffer on duty at the pool allegedly left, and a man went on duty, and almost let other patrons, who had arrived after the witness, access the pool before him.

Once he was inside, the

man stated that he sorted through his swim bag, which contained his swim trunks; a diving mask; two towels, one of which was printed with an Aztec pattern; and several neckties.

Clear skin on Asian trips

LOS ANGELES — A local man reportedly had dinner tonight with a former colleague and several students. The woman stated that she was going to Vietnam for the year-end holiday break, on dates that overlapped with the man's trip. The man allegedly told the woman that his skin always clears up when traveling in Southeast Asia, and stated that he felt he was "quite eloquent."

Car wheel nearly detached

Leftover from past service

LOS ANGELES — Double-parked on a quiet street, a man alleged today that he was "working on a crossword puzzle." When a car pulled away from the curb, the man took the parking space, and noticed that his right front wheel had almost fallen off.

The man stated that he considered calling a tow truck, but when he looked closer, crouching to see under the front end of the car, he saw that the detached wheel was actually something left behind by a tow truck or a mechanic in the past. His own wheel was reportedly "fine."

• • • • • •

Teetotaler imbibes cocktail

"Forgot" abstinence

LOS ANGELES — When his roommate prepared him a manhattan cocktail described as "glammy," a local man reportedly sat on the living room floor to drink it. Only after he felt "buzzed" did the man remember that he doesn't drink.

Apartment window safety concerns

CITY — A local man reported today that his city-center apartment had no safety bars on the windows, despite being located on the fifth floor. The windows were described as the size of full-length doors, and one of the windows, in the corner and facing north, was allegedly located "at the right side of the sofa." The man stated that he looked out

the window, down at the street, and claimed that "It gave me vertigo even to look."

• • • • • •

Drinking before fighting

LOCAL — Reports tonight indicate that a group of friends sang their motto before they got into fights.

The motto was allegedly "We drink before we fight." The purpose was reportedly that the drinking was so that they wouldn't remember the fighting.

Woman with lengthy name celebrated in song

"Fast, twangy" country music beat

CITY — A local man reported tonight that he witnessed a man and woman pull up in a car. The vehicle's audio system was allegedly playing a song that the witness described as "humorous" and "set to a fast twangy country beat." The man related the song's lyrics:

> I saw him drive up with his new girlfriend in town;
> Her name is Jennifer Ruth Mary Gail Tina Annette Suzie Louise Brown.

* * * * * *

Gruesome injuries in Hollywood truck crash

Emergency call repeatedly interrupted

LOS ANGELES — Riding the bus this morning on his way to work at his office on Hollywood Boulevard, a local man reported that several other passengers on the bus were foreign tourists reportedly searching for the offices of Céline Dion's gynecologist. The tourists allegedly saw a sign in the third-floor window of a building along the boulevard, and disembarked at the corner of Hollywood and Orange Drive.

From the courtyard of the office building at that corner, the man alleges that a small red truck veered out of control. He stated that he could see the driver, described as "Latino," whom he theorized had either fallen asleep or had a heart attack. The pickup slowly backed up toward the witness, who described jumping out of the way. The truck struck the man's boss as she was entering the building through the glass doors, and she got several large shards of glass wedged in her body.

One of the shards was described as "bisecting" her hand, and another was lodged in her liver. The man stated that he attempted to pull a couple of the shards out, but they were solidly wedged in her flesh. The woman allegedly tried to brace one of the shards on his hand in order to pull it out, which caused him concern that he would get cut.

The man stated that he "got her calmed down" and then called 911. He was unable to complete the call because the build-ing management's executive interrupted the call to ask what was going on. The man reportedly hung up and dialed again, but the building executive interrupted the call each time. Finally the man stated that he threatened the executive: "If you don't stop doing this, I'll tell the cops you obstructed a 911 emergency call."

The call finally went through, but the voice that answered was described as that of a young boy. The man allegedly said, "Who's this?" to which the boy said, "Bill." The witness asked, "Bill who?" The boy replied, "I can't believe you don't recognize your own nephew." The youth was reportedly at the hospital visiting someone.

· · · · · ·

Whirlwind romance marred by "crazy" neighbor

LOS ANGELES — A man was reportedly introduced to a "great guy" at a party by a woman that he didn't know. The pair reportedly walked around the local neighborhood, and often felt in danger, but subsequently fell in love and moved in together. At their new residence, one of the neighbors was described as "scary" and "crazy" as he brandished several knives, repeatedly flicking them open and closed in his hand. The witness stated that the neighbor seemed "unbalanced."

• • • • • •

Chewed-up ibuprofen reused

LOCAL — Reports tonight indicate that a man took a handful of ibuprofen tablets, even though he'd already taken some earlier. The man allegedly chewed up a "huge mouthful" of the tablets, but then spat some back, walking away from his friend to conceal his actions.

His friend then reportedly told him to bring the partially chewed tablets back, and put them in the bottle, even though they were wet with saliva, as she would be able to use them later.

Porn viewing in family home

LOCAL — A man reported tonight that he attempted to watch a porn video in his parents' bedroom while the rest of his family was nearby in the living room. The house was described as spacious, with linen and light-colored wood, reminiscent of the Getty Center in Los Angeles.

Prework house visit leads to messy incident

LOCAL — Reports tonight indicate that a man visited the home that a college friend was sharing with a woman and her girlfriend. Dropping in before they were all due to go to work, the man stated that he briefly met the two other women, and said that was leaving, but then stayed with his friend as she got ready for work.

The man and his friend each took a shower, and he stated that he could hear the other two residents talking cheerfully in another bathroom as they got ready for work. Concerned that he might be "putting them out," while talking to his friend, the man allegedly shit on the bathroom floor, then turned his back in order to hide the mess, and scooped it up, and flushed it.

Objects dropped in pool

LOS ANGELES — On his way to work this morning, a Los Angeles man reports that "things kept falling in the swimming pool." He allegedly dropped things into the pool accidentally, which people in the pool would sometimes hand back to him. "It had a good meaning, though, like a baptism," he stated. Among the items to take

the plunge were a long black spoon and a Model T car.

・ ・ ・ ・ ・ ・

Bedtime delayed

Tryst with "hot blond" planned

LOCAL — Reports tonight indicate that a work colleague and a man described as "a hot married blond" were staying over at the family home of a local man. The witness reports that in an attempt to hook up with the blond, the pair cleared boxes off one of the twin beds, only to discover the man's sibling already asleep in the bed under the boxes.

The man reported that "bedtime kept getting delayed," in part at the hands of the man's mother. Finally a plan was formulated to clean the room. The man's brother, angry at being roused from his slumber, assisted in the project, but allegedly insulted the man's work colleague, described as "technically obese," by telling him, "You should have stopped eating sooner." The man reportedly said, "You can't talk to my friend that way." The brother then apologized, and the man said that he explained away his brother's behavior by describing his "Christian thing."

The man stated that he then agreed with the blond to sneak off outside in the light of dawn with a blanket, and the man agreed, even though he was described as dubious about the plan. The blond asked the man if he had his wife's phone number written down anywhere.

House with "many dangers"

Tiger mauling reported

FLORIDA — Reports tonight indicate that the old house in tropical Florida, owned by a local man, was the site of "many dangers." The man stated that these dangers included tigers. One of the man's elementary school peers allegedly got mauled. The house contained secret passages, and residents reportedly avoided the tiger by traveling the "women's rooms route."

. . . . . .

Protest scene in bank

Chants, sit-in, "mouthiness"

LOS ANGELES — Waiting in line at a local bank, a man stated that the line was moving "really slow." When he was next in line for the teller, somehow six people cut in front of him. The man then allegedly started complaining loudly, and with other customers organized a chant of "ca ... shier! ca ... shier!" along with a sit-down protest.

The man stated that his next chant, "Break the bank! Break the bank!" was less successful. He allegedly rattled off "a whole monologue" about it being Christmas, "Don't you think we have better things to do," and so on.

Finally reaching the teller window, the man stated that he realized he had made a mistake on his deposit slip, and had to start again. He admitted that he was being "mouthy" with the teller.

In the line behind the witness, a man wearing a trench coat allegedly got too close, so the man faked that the man had broken his spine. "I grabbed at the teller's window and cried for help."

. . . . . .

Different incarnations of hotel seen

Black-and-white gives way to color

LOS ANGELES — A local man reports walking around "Old Downtown" Los Angeles with a companion who pointed out the Chicagoland Hotel and its bright neon sign. The man described the scene as "black-and-white" and stated that both he and the other man were wearing classic film noir–style suits.

Later, the witness's companion pointed out the modern incarnation of the hotel as it looked in later years. The sign read

"CLI" and the man stated that "it was in color now." The witness stated that he thought his companion was clever to have recognized it.

. . . . . .

Small sink the focus of party

CITY — Attending a basement house party tonight, a local man reported that his coworker "was drink-ing too much." The witness stated that he spent a long time washing his face in the small sink in the bathroom while chatting with a British film actor. The woman eventually asked if she could "butt in" so that she could rinse out her blouse. The man stated that his beard had become a mottled blotchy green color. He also allegedly witnessed a lesbian kiss in the doorway.

· · · · · ·

Twin requirements revised

LOCAL — A man reported tonight that his brother outlined the new requirements for twins: all twins must now be male-female. His brother stated that his name was now legally Roderickina instead of Roderick, and that his mail was now addressed to "Ms."

· · · · · ·

Late for reunion, talks to no one

Shirt changed in parking lot

CITY — A local man reported tonight that he attended the ten-year reunion of his part-time student job along with his parents. His mother reportedly decided to come at the last minute, but then didn't.

The man stated that it took a long time for him to get ready in the parking lot, and that he "discreetly" changed his shirt. Because the event was only scheduled from 6 to 7 p.m., his father went in ahead. The witness allegedly saw several people that he knew, but didn't talk to them.

When he finally got inside, the caterers were cleaning up, and the event's stragglers were just leaving. The man stated that he found his father sitting and talking to two "old guys." He allegedly put his arm around his father's neck and told him, "I didn't see anyone I knew."

As the pair were leaving the event, the man stated that a woman stared at him, as if she knew him, but he didn't talk to her. He alleged that he and his father walked out with two of his college roommates, and neither one had changed much, but he didn't talk to them.

Hummingbird attack

LOCAL —While collaborating with a renowned alien investigator, an area man claimed that he was assaulted by hummingbirds. "They were injecting my shoulders and neck with their long bills," the man explained. The experience was described as "very painful."

· · · · · ·

Assaulted by children, retaliates with butter

Avoids police in garden

TOKAI REGION, JAPAN — On a pedestrian shopping excursion, a man alleged that two small boys came up and pulled on his T-shirt, pulling him along, "as if I wasn't even there." Because the children weren't paying attention, the man admitted that he rubbed butter on the back of one child's neck, and on the shirt of the other boy.

Walking away, the man reportedly crossed the street at an uncontrolled intersection and went to his own street. Near the bottom of the street, he saw several women gathering, so he went up a flight of stairs into an outdoor garden. A woman sitting in the garden allegedly "completely ignored me."

The man waited in the garden for several minutes for the women on the street to disperse, but more of them gathered. Realizing he'd dropped one of his papers, a flyer, the man then decided to leave, and grabbed his flyer from the bush it was resting on, described as "either a camelia or a hyacinth."

The women on the street reportedly didn't see the man as he stepped out into the open, and the man stated that a police car had arrived. As he walked toward his house, the man stated that he hoped he

wouldn't be mobbed by the women, and rehearsed his explanation in Japanese about how the boys had essentially assaulted him.

Restaurant booking requires labor

Men's room, mall explored

QUEBEC, CANADA — On vacation with his roommates, a man visiting the area states that they checked into a hotel. The man subsequently went upstairs to the "vast" restaurant to reserve a table. The woman staffing the restaurant desk asked the man to set his own table because "she was so busy."

The man reported that he set the table for four, because he thought a friend might join them later. He subsequently walked around the restaurant, studying landmarks so that he would be able to explain where the table was on the phone later. He stated that near the restaurant's main entrance was a meat bar, like a salad bar but where diners cut their own meat off roasts.

The witness subsequently went to the men's room, but because he was allegedly not wearing shoes, he was forced to tread carefully to ensure that his socks and pant legs didn't touch the puddles of urine on the floor. The restroom cubicles were described as "like corrals," with open fencing around them.

Subsequently wandering into the adjacent shopping mall, the man stated that he looked at women's clothing. One of his roommates then called to ask about the "French deal" they had arranged for later at a different hotel. His roommate allegedly stated that the deal included a room, dinner, and a show. The witness stated that he didn't know what his roommate was talking about at first, but then he remembered; he had planned to arrange a similar deal at this hotel.

In the mall he then spotted an ad campaign for shoes, where the shoes are the colorful accent to an outfit, in colors like mustard yellow with clothing that was uniformly black and gray.

· · · · · ·

Issue with resizing car

Brakes fail, causing crash

ON THE ROAD — Reports tonight indicate that a man undertook a road trip with five friends, after his flight was canceled when the plane he was scheduled to fly on had a small accident before departing. Because he was going for only two days, the man stated that he wasn't able to extend the trip.

The six travelers rode in a large Land Rover that was described as having "various problems." At one point the vehicle shrank when one of the passengers used a shrink remote control. They managed to resize the vehicle again, but the man stated that it was hard to judge the exact size, and "we did it by checking how much leg room we had."

The vehicle also lost braking power, when the man and one other passenger were aboard, allegedly rolling back-ward down a mountain dirt road. "I pressed the brake," the man stated, "but we kept going, pushing the car behind us." When the man shifted the transmission into gear, the vehicle slowed down, but the car they had been pushing then rolled out of control and flipped into the dusty ravine beside the road. One of his traveling companions, described as "a guy that I liked," was left dead in the dust.

Later, the group was at a train station in Japan, watching the shinkansen bullet train pass by from the platform. A double-decker shinkansen with a red stripe down the side stopped at the platform, and the man described seeing people inside, seated on tatami mats, eating and "hanging out." Aboard the train, one of the man's traveling companions allegedly took some food—a cookie—from the cabin of a family of tourists without asking. The family promptly closed their cabin door.

• • • • • •

Crowds gather for end of world

Team colors worn

LOCAL — Alleging that the end of the world was "nigh," a local man reported tonight that people started massing at a castle. The situation was described as "getting worse" as people milled around, and power shifted politically.

Finally the man was able to get into a set of underground rooms along with several others, including the cartoon character Tin Tin, still in cartoon form. Outside, people allegedly started falling over each other. Many of them were described as wearing "striped UK team hats and scarves."

Controversial film portrayal of Churchill

Gender "overrated"

OTTAWA, CANADA — Reports tonight indicate that a dramatic film about British wartime prime minister Winston Churchill has seen pushback. The film was aimed at a gay audience and portrayed Churchill as gay. Critics panned the film, claiming Churchill was straight, but the film's defenders stated that "It's a movie" and "Gender is overrated." One dramatic scene in the film was described as a "long, slow walk" through a Nazi rally where Hitler was speaking on a stage. The rally was held on Parliament Hill in Ottawa, with the Parliament as the backdrop.

Solitude in mountain cabin

IN THE MOUNTAINS — A man reported tonight that he was staying in a cabin "in a high place." The structure was described as having lots of windows and heavy curtains. The man stated that he locked the doors in order to maintain his peace and solitude, but that some old people dropped by to play cards. He allegedly opened the transom to get fresh air. The doors and locks were described as "like in Europe": cheap and thin and old.

Rehired for student job 20 years later

Misses bus, shoes scuffed, late arrival

CITY — A local man reported today that he was hired to work at his part-time college job after a gap of twenty years. He stated that he was unable to find the shuttle bus to get to the work site, that his shoes were badly scuffed, and that he was over an hour late on his first day of work.

Castle restoration tour

Cameras attached to head

SCOTLAND — Reports today indicate that a man looked around a castle with cameras attached to his head so that people could follow his commentary about restoring the structure. The man looked at the previously restored wall where a car had driven through the bricks; the garage walls and doors; and an abandoned outdoor space between a wall

and a fence that was about five feet wide.

A police officer reportedly "hassled" the man to leave the premises, but the man was able to produce some documentation as evidence that he was allowed to be there. The man states that he subsequently "hit on" the police officer.

· · · · · ·

Competency questioned at grocery checkout

First-day performance "really slow"

LOCAL — Reports today indicate that a local man was recently employed as a checkout clerk at an old-fashioned grocery store. The man described his performance on his first day as "really slow." Ringing up an elderly customer's purchases "seemed to take forever," to the point that the customer finally just went home. The man stated that his boss was "putting pressure on."

When the next shift arrived, the man stated that his replacement was a young "pretty" guy, allegedly with a bad attitude, who implied that the witness was incompetent.

Reunion attendees dramatically changed

Unknown offspring revealed

CITY — A man reported tonight that he attended a reunion of his college part-time job. The event was held in a big hall with raw wood fittings, described as "like at a campground."

The other attendees reportedly had changed dramatically, to the point of being unrecognizable. One former colleague allegedly brushed the man off. The man's parents were also in attendance.

In the back room, the man discovered that a program had been printed for the reunion event, including a biography of him. The bio stated that the man had two children: a daughter that he knew about and a son that he'd had at age twelve that he didn't know about. There was a photo of the boy with his adoptive gay dads in another city. The man stated that the youth "looked like me." The man stated that he had a "creepy, ill" feeling that he'd done something as significant as sire a child but couldn't remember doing so, or had blocked it out.

Actor goes shopping

Vague interaction reported

LOS ANGELES — Working in a local store, a West Hollywood man alleges that a well-known female actor came in and began a conversation with him. "She told me some story about some people, and then asked my advice," the man explained. "I hadn't been listening very closely, so I had to diplomatically ask her to repeat the details again." The man also claims there was an unspoken indication that the actor might employ him to teach her English.

Airport hotel camera work

Kimonos, saris worn

LAX — A man reported tonight that he was assigned the same task as a work colleague, and wore cameras attached to his head. The man allegedly parked his car illegally on a ramp at the airport. When he returned later, the vehicle was still there, but he found a note under the wiper, written by himself, instructing him to move the car.

The man and his colleague then went into a hotel room in the terminal, where they changed into kimonos, and the hotel staff working in the room were wearing saris. The staffers were described as "really short, like four feet tall."

At one point the man gave his colleague a hug, which allegedly led one of the staffers to assume they wanted privacy for an intimate encounter. That wasn't the case, but they didn't correct her assump-tion, and let her leave.

· · · · · ·

Time-travel to 1967 theme park

Host wearing muumuu

LOS ANGELES — A man reportedly time-traveled to 1967, and stated that he read a magazine, "trying to soak up the historical vibe." A former work colleague was also there, and the pair traveled out to a school meeting that was held on a hill. From the hilltop they could see a discount clothing store, and the woman went back to visit the store.

The man went to a Flintstones-themed theme park called Hawaiian Gardens and stated that he "loved the period stuff." He remembered driving past the theme park with a boyfriend in his own time, but by then it was an abandoned ruin. The man stated that the theme park had a theme song playing on a television screen, and reported the lyrics:

Come with us
Emotion's got a name
Come with us

The man reportedly spoke to a tall woman described as "somewhat overweight" and with short blond hair, wearing a white muumuu with the Hawaiian Gardens information and characters written all over it. The man asked if he could read her other knee, and wondered whether it would be weird in the 1967 context to do so, and if other people in the cafeteria would stare at them.

Down Under tour

Car crashed at furniture store

AUSTRALIA — A visitor to the southern nation today reported that he was traveling around with a man he occasionally hooked up with, and met some of his friends. The visitor alleged that "we kissed once, but mostly we didn't." The man reportedly rented a red car, and then crashed it by driving off a ramp at a furniture store. Another friend joined him in "try-ing to pretend the car back into existence," but it allegedly didn't work.

· · · · · ·

No toilet in London flat

Red alligator boots worn

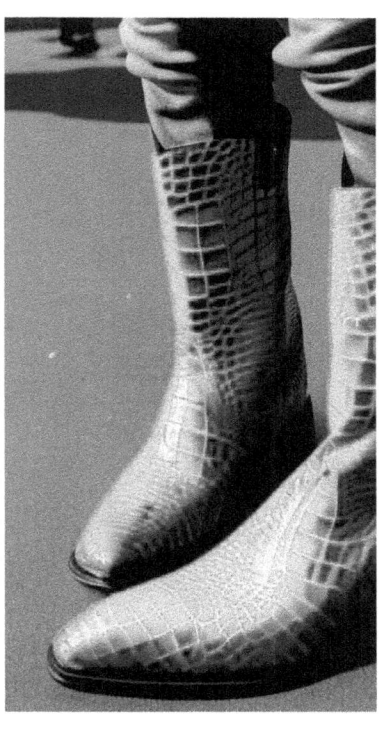

LONDON — A visitor to the British capital described staying at the home of a local resident, a U.S. expatriate. The pair reportedly "hung out," and when the man "went out for something," he wore alligator boots that were described as "fire-engine red."

On his return, his host explained that she was going out to use the toilet. She was dressed in a white shift and carried a roll of toilet paper.

Japan "changed a lot"

Described as "less interesting"

TOKAI REGION, JAPAN — Returning to Japan after an absence of many years, a former resident described collecting colorful flyers for various events and festivals. The man stated that the country had changed a lot, and didn't seem as interesting or as welcoming as it once had.

When he visited a bookstore described as "an old haunt," the man alleged that there weren't as many books as there used to be.

Outside he noticed a former work colleague on the street, watching an event. The woman acknowledged him but allegedly "didn't want to connect." Generally, the man stated, people didn't want to connect.

. . . . . .

Crush attends dinner party
Stroll in mythical hills considered

IN THE COUNTRYSIDE — Reports tonight indicate that a man hosted a dinner party for two former neighbors, a woman that he didn't know, and a man described as "kind of my type." As the dinner ended and the evening progressed, the other guests departed, leaving only the host and the man he was interested in.

The witness stated that he then took his guest over to his father's house to introduce him, and considered taking a walk in the hill country in the valleys around his father's house, but the sun was nearing the horizon in the northwest, and it would soon be dark. When pressed for details on the hill country, the man stated that it was "mythical" and existed "only in old dreams."

Theater seating bungled
Patron, staff "rude"

CITY — A local man reported that the staff at an upscale theater had given away the seats that were to be occupied by his father, brother, and himself. The man was allegedly "rude" to the staffers, and reports that "they were rude back."

Dinner guides met with violence

LOS ANGELES — Reports tonight indicate that a man was staying at the home of a local psychic, but that the home was actually a large modern hotel suite. The man was due for dinner at the psychic's house for "a special event." When two men entered the hotel suite to take the witness to dinner, the man admits that "I slammed their heads against the wall" and then laid out their unconscious bodies, one of them on a lounger by the pool in his underpants. The man stated that "I think I had an accomplice at that point."

When he finally arrived at the dinner event, the host was described as "cool" about his late arrival, but the other guests were gone, and the staff was clearing the dishes. The man stated that he then left town because of the assaults he had committed.

Bag missing at airport

Staffer in "hot yellow" Civic

NARITA AIRPORT, JAPAN — Reports tonight from Japan's principal aviation gateway indicate that a man could not find his luggage. "I looked for the plane," the man stated, "and I looked for the baggage office." Finally he called a friend to pick him up.

An airport staffer reportedly helped the pair search for the missing bag, and eventually located it. The witness stated that "someone had put my bowling ball in a mesh bag." The airport staffer then drove the pair and several others to the train station in his Honda Civic, described as "hot yellow."

· · · · · ·

Van employed to move

Power-steering belts "shriek"

LOCAL — Reports tonight indicate that a local man moved house, using a van, with the assistance of his brother and a niece. His brother drove the van while he sat in the passenger seat and the niece sat

in back, behind the passenger's seat. It was night, and there was reportedly three inches of snow on the ground.

When the trio pulled into a driveway that allegedly "looked like the one at the swimming pool," they found the man's boxes stacked in a single ten-foot-high column. The niece reportedly stated "I love winter" as the witness climbed out of the van. Because the van was a bit far from the boxes, his brother moved the vehicle closer, backing in. The witness reported that as he maneuvered the vehicle, the power-steering belts "shrieked" all the while.

UCLA turn lanes blocked

Body found on campus

LOS ANGELES — Reports from the city's Westwood neighborhood tonight indicate that a man attempted to turn into the UCLA campus on his bicycle. At the front of the turn lanes, however, there was allegedly a stalled car in both of the lanes. The man stated that he then zipped past all the waiting vehicles on his bicycle, along the side.

The man then allegedly entered one of the red-brick rowhouses on campus that was slated for renovation. A dead body had been found in the building, and the man stated that he went "way up on the roof" to listen to the investigation.

Zombies run rampant

Animals, people infected

IN THE COUNTRYSIDE — A local man reported tonight that a virus was spreading that turned animals and people into zombies. The man and others allegedly spent a lot of time fighting off zombies, first the animals and later people. When he visited the rural home of his brother and sister-in-law, they refused to believe that zombies were real, and opened the door to step outside. The pair became infected, and zombies allegedly got inside the house.

Commandos bunking in hotel basement

CITY — A man reported tonight that he was part of a commando group who wore heavy winter clothing and harnesses. The group was reportedly bunking in the basement of a large old hotel. The man stated that "there were lots of us together" and alleges that he remembers walking up the stairs over all the coats.

Old blues song on French road trip

Mystifying lyrics interpreted

FRANCE — A man reported today driving around the French countryside with a friend and her young son. The trio stopped at a café, and listened to what was described as "an old blues song" in English. Because the song's lyrics were not clearly enunciated, the man interpreted them:

> I wouldn't have taken that brace of goats from last season.

. . . . . .

Two robots alleged

LOCAL — A man reported tonight that he thought there were two robots. The machines were described as "metallic" with "Lego-like" features. As it turned out, the male robot had just "put on a wig and used a high voice."

. . . . . .

Wrong-way driver averts crash

Uses "cop shortcut" in hilly terrain

LOS ANGELES — Reports tonight indicate that a local man was driving a BMW convertible, with the top up, on a divided highway. The vehicle allegedly belonged to the man's friend, and in the backseat was the owner's mother. The man stated that he pulled out of the median, but that he was "going the wrong way," in lane 1 of three or four lanes.

The man managed to avert a crash by taking "a cop shortcut" to the right, through the bush and over gravel—the terrain was described as "hilly country" and the road curvy—to get on the correct side of the highway.

Water walking at mall

Sobriety "on hold"

CITY — At a local mall today a man reported walking in the water in front of a long row of shops. The water was described as waist- to shoulder-deep. The man stated that he was walking for exercise, but that he then decided to put his sobriety "on hold" and get at drink. Walking in the opposite direction, the man reportedly got

into a competition with another water pedestrian, and the two were allegedly struck by a large wave.

Immigration hassles

Tax documents coded in vegetables

LOS ANGELES — A foreign resident of Japan reported today that he spent "hours and hours" with a Japanese immigration officer trying to get into the country. He allegedly showed the officer tax forms that were coded in carrots and other vegetables.

The man stated that he was wearing red high-heeled strappy sandals and walking around Union Station in Downtown Los Angeles to get the material organized. The man stated that the situation was "annoying, because when she'd been a new young officer, she'd let me come and go without hassle."

The officer allegedly made him write down where he'd worked for any amount over ¥79 (about $0.60), and wanted to check that he hadn't been paid much more that year. The man stated that he wrote down the names of all his employers, but couldn't remember the name of one, because it had been over two years.

. . . . . .

Interlopers use car to look for car
Siblings scream at each other

LOS ANGELES — A local man reported tonight that three men, described as Filipino, were driving his car around looking for their own car while he and his brother sat in the backseat. The man stated that they were driving around the Hollywood neighborhood but that it was also a lightly populated beachfront area.

The man states that he "tried to regain control" but that the driver pulled into a parking lot, where they got "stuck" beside a big truck and behind an old Volkswagen Beetle, described as "tiny" and tan-brown in color. Finally the woman driving the Beetle moved the car.

The man's brother then allegedly screamed in his ear that "we should go into this store." The man stated that he screamed back, "You have to stop screaming."

. . . . . .

Hanging from 40-story building
Pizza thrown

LOS ANGELES — A local man described hanging on the side of a forty-story building with two other people, described as a blond woman and her boyfriend. The woman's children were allegedly across the alley, hanging from a different building at the same height.

The trio allegedly ordered pizza, and several slices "went flying" as the woman tossed them to the others. The man stated that he managed to catch a slice, and proceeded to eat it, but that he couldn't quite heave himself up to safety.

· · · · · · ·

Time with woman who discovered pi

Restaurant visitor "difficult"

LOS ANGELES — An area resident reported tonight that he was "hanging out" in a restaurant with the woman who discovered pi. [*Editor's note:* This article refers to the number π, the mathematical constant that describes the ratio of a circle's circumference to its diameter.]

A young business owner, described as having short red hair and wearing a lime-green skirt suit, visited the restaurant. The man stated that "I knew she was a difficult person."

Man mostly able to avoid extended family

Relatives gather at grove of trees

LOCAL — On a recent visit to his family's home, a local man stated that he "managed to avoid the scion purposefully." When the man entered the garden shed, he noticed that two dune buggies drove by outside, headed southbound. One of the vehicles was white, and the other purple. Three of the man's nieces were allegedly standing up in the back of the purple one.

To avoid his relatives, the man stated that he went through the shed and up the garden path. The shed door had been open, and the man closed it, then opened it again, leaving it ajar in just the way it had been when he arrived. The man allegedly saw his sister-in-law through the porch window of her house, and spotted another sibling's Yukon parked in the yard, but managed to avoid them both.

Because it was Christmas Day, the man's extended family were gath-

ered at the house, but the structure more closely resembled a grove of trees. The man's mother was seen on the left, up a little hill, surrounded by a few of her loved ones. She was described as "large-bellied and a little skin-blotchy, but happy."

The man's father sat nearby, reading, with his sister. The witness stated that "For a long delightful moment, I went unnoticed," but then his father extended a casual warm greeting.

Actor aids with bank forms

TOKAI REGION, JAPAN — A man reported tonight that a well-known Hollywood actor assisted him in making a bank deposit. The branch was closed, but the pair were "in there using a desk." The deposit forms were described as "extremely complex."

"Major" typos alleged

Remote work at family home

LOCAL — A local man reports that because his mother and siblings were all out at work today, he "hung out" at their place to do his own remote work. He allegedly sent an email to four people at the company he worked for, explaining what he was doing, but claimed that he then later found "major typos" in his email message.

Meeting attendees visit

Late-night street closures lock down neighborhood

WEST HOLLYWOOD, CALIF. — Walking home after a meeting late at night, a local resident reported that he was near the corner of Fairfax Avenue and Santa Monica Boulevard when another meeting attendee phoned him. The man wasn't far behind, and caught up so that they could talk in person.

The man pointed out that all the streets were

closed, so that no one could leave the neighborhood. He reportedly asked the witness if six or seven guys from the meeting could hang out at his place until the police reopened the streets. The witness stated that he said, "Sure, as long as they're quiet; my roommate is sleeping."

The man stated that he hadn't noticed the blocked streets or the fact that there was "zero traffic," but described the neighborhood as "quiet, dark, and eerie."

Evening drive strikes pedestrian

Public meeting called

AUSTRALIA — A U.S. visitor was reportedly driving with an Australian friend tonight on a busy street. The man allegedly opened the passenger door a few inches, accidentally hitting a young woman named Nikki in the head. As they got farther away from the site of the incident, the reactions of people on the sidewalk became more severe.

Finally the incident led to a meeting in an auditorium. The man states that at the meeting, he publicly admitted what he'd done, and that he found it scary that the woman might have brain damage.

Man wakes up between lives

Life as mouse remembered

LOCAL — Reports tonight indicate that a local man woke up on a beach between lives. Previously he had lived in a beachside kingdom as a mouse, in a big old house, under a threatening ruler. The man stated that as a mouse, he wasn't aware of the reincarnational nature

of reality. He stated that as a mouse, he succeeded in his quest "to be liberated," and woke up human on the beach.

With him on the beach were a high school friend, described as now having short wavy blond hair, and an unknown man. The man stated that the others couldn't remember their previous incarnations, even though he clearly remembered his life as a mouse.

· · · · · ·

Hummingbirds spotted

Carafe employed as feeder

LOS ANGELES — On discovering that hummingbirds were flitting around outside the kitchen window today, a local man reportedly built a makeshift bird feeder. He covered his roommate's carafe in fine mesh, then filled it with sugar water and inverted it. The top was described as "white ceramic."

ER visit leads to psych eval

Man labeled "low priority"

LOS ANGELES — While out cycling, a local man decided to drop into a hospital for a checkup. He reportedly entered the ER, and found it "very quiet." When the staff found that he didn't have an emergency, they allegedly performed a psych evaluation on the man. The psych evaluation reportedly consisted of finding Los Angeles on a series of small world maps.

A patient in the waiting room asked the duty nurse whether the witness was "on the return list." The man asked the nurse what that meant. The nurse reportedly explained that it meant "low priority." The man wandered around the hospital and reportedly considered "bailing," because it was going to take "all day."

Mother's actions cause bee swarm

LOCAL — While visiting the home of his parents, a man reported tonight that he spent time with them in the garden. At one point his mother allegedly "did something" that caused bees to swarm around the man's hands and the back of his neck. He stated that he ran around, left and right, attempting to gently blow them off. The bees were described as unusually small, although "some were normal size." Eventually the swarm dispersed.

Talk over professor's point

Brother coddled

LOCAL — Talking to his professor along with another student, a man reported tonight that the professor made a point using "an old saying." At the same time that the professor was speaking, the man's brother was allegedly telling his own story, and the man stated that he missed the professor's words.

At that point he reportedly asked his brother to be quiet, and his brother became "miffed" and had to be coddled afterward.

Toilets aboard *Titanic* "very busy, very public"

Ship manages to dock in New York

NORTH ATLANTIC OCEAN — Tonight a man described traveling on the passenger ship *Titanic*. Even though he was in first class, the man allegedly couldn't

find a toilet: "at least not a men's toilet with a private stall." The toilets on the ship were described as "either very public, very busy, or on public display." When the ship docked in New York, the man stated that he studied the faces of some of the passengers with the awareness that in an alternate reality, these people would be dead. The man explained that standing on the pier during disembarkation, he studied one of the female passengers, who had short hair and was "a little chubby," with "Anglo-Irish" features.

Critic defaces art for sale

Adds new paint, pencil marks

LOS ANGELES — A local man reported today that he and his boyfriend went shopping for art after inheriting some money. The man stated that a high school friend "tagged along," and that she "dissed" the art. The woman also allegedly added new paint strokes and pencil marks to some of the artworks "as a test." One artwork was described as a modern abstract grid, and another as a folding-board world map from a game.

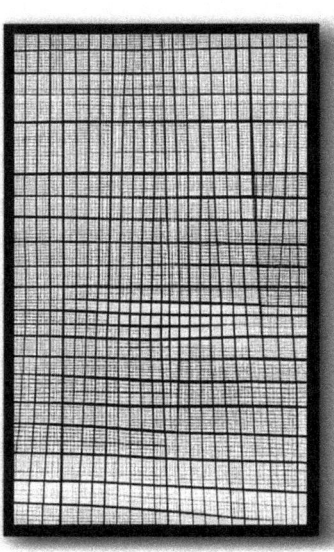

Dirty industrial space toured

Dark film on windows

CITY — Reports tonight indicate that a man was touring an industrial space inside a warehouse building, described as "extremely dirty." The man stated that there were maggots around the sink. He washed his hands elsewhere, but when he turned on the lever for the water, a hose fed into a giant fire extinguisher behind the sink, causing it to "hiss and rattle."

The man was allegedly able to see through the dark film on the unit's windows into the outdoor mall outside, located just a few feet below. He stated that he could also see into neighboring offices, and saw people working, but their windows were coated with dark film too.

Two cats appeared, allegedly "wanting affection," and though they were assumed to be strays, both looked well-fed. As the man was preparing to leave, another person arrived, looking at the space as a potential warehouse for his fabric rolls. The man's boyfriend and another friend were reportedly with him, waiting in the hall.

Dinner aboard moving platform

Difficult hill ascent

LOS ANGELES — A man reported today that he participated in a dinner that was held on a platform that was being towed into and out of a valley. One of the other guests was described as "a Maine lobsterman." On the way up the hill out of the valley, the man states that he closed his eyes and held tightly to two large plastic containers "so that they wouldn't blow away." At one point the platform was also towed down Hollywood Boulevard, but it was described as "like Hong Kong."

* * * * * *

Police uncover contract killer

Crooks "shockingly irrational"

LOS ANGELES — A man reported tonight that a television detective was working undercover as a hired killer that "wiped out office workers on contract." The police managed to catch the person who'd put out the contract, but then someone else hired the undercover detective.

Another police detective, described as having an eye infection, was reportedly investigating. The witness reported tagging along with the detective, and stated that he was "shocked at how irrational crooks are." The contract killer allegedly identified his targets by writing down their office phone extensions.

In the heat of the investigation there were allegedly some rank-and-file cop complaints because they had to make warning signs to be posted on the street, partly by cutting and pasting lettering from the newspaper and by writing on paper with pens.

• • • • • •

Passport defaced

"Official documents" taped on

SAN FRANCISCO — A man reported tonight that he was waiting at a counter in the airport to get service, but the staff "fastidiously ignored me." The man stated that he then walked away, toward the gate, and "of course they sent a cop after me." Back at the counter, the staff allegedly took the man's new passport "for a long time." When the staff eventually returned his passport, it was allegedly covered with "childish paper drawings" taped over most of the front and back. The man stated that he wanted to rip them off, but the staff said they were official documents and thus had to stay on.

Power failure, car towed

Tea served with "red bits"

PASADENA, CALIF. — man reported today that he parked on a street in the City of Churches and went into a Trader Joe's, where he had table service, including tea. The tea was served in a filter, like coffee, but was described as "colorful, like trail mix, with red bits in it."

The shop then reportedly suffered a power failure,

and the situation became confusing. The man stated that the server said he'd get back to him, but it was very slow, so he walked out. His car, a 1974 Plymouth, had allegedly been towed because they were setting up for the farmers market. The man states that he attempted to track down the parking meter patrol, but that they were "elusive."

Journalist handles hotel booking

LOS ANGELES — A man reported tonight that a PBS journalist assisted him in making a hotel reservation. The woman allegedly placed a phone call to the hotel and "skillfully and quickly" went through the options, and negotiated the room rate.

Mushroom cloud spotted

Witnesses panicked

WYOMING OR SOUTH DAKOTA — Reports today from a ranch in either Wyoming or South Dakota indicate that an airplane flew over at an extremely high speed, leaving a smoke trail across the entire sky. In the distance the witness stated that he saw a mushroom cloud, and attempted to phone loved ones. On the ranch he alleged that people were "running around," and he attempted to sit down inside the ranch house.

· · · · · ·

ATM trouble, new construction in Japan

Mac-and-cheese lunch on the return walk

TOKAI REGION, JAPAN — Returning to a school where he had worked two decades earlier, a man discovered that he was on the schedule to teach on Thursday the 21st at 7 p.m. He met several of the new teachers who were there "hanging around," and noticed in the calendar the name of his current boyfriend. Wondering if they'd ever met before, the man stated that he made a mental note to ask him. The man stated that he considered attempting to make friends, but that it seemed like too much for the moment.

The man then decided to put some of his money in a different ATM, in a different bank account. The machine kept his card along with a twenty-dollar bill, then displayed images of the street outside. The man took that as a cue to exit the bank, and outside claimed that he saw a woman wearing a trench coat take his card. He allegedly confronted her, and saw that the card didn't look like the one he'd lost. Eventually the man got his card back from the machine, which allegedly "kept playing commercials," but he was unable to get the money from the machine.

Back at his school, the administrators gave him "about forty-five dollars in mixed bills" as a refund for a project that wasn't going to work. The man stated that he had lots of U.S. cash but no local money, and thought he should obtain some. He reportedly decided then not to open a new account, as of the two that he already had, one was "low." He deposited a check for "about $336" into the account.

Walking up the street, the man reportedly went past his old house, and past several food carts, then up a hill and past a park, into a valley where the house was. The end of the road was covered in iron plates, which the man stated hadn't been there before. Near the iron plates the man allegedly slipped on the grass and into a "shadow hole," reportedly the result of a plumbing problem. A man standing "twenty or thirty yards away" allegedly looked at the witness and possibly recognized him.

The witness stated that the Victorian girls school next door to his former house appeared, from a distance, to have new metalwork on the towers. He stated that he got no closer than "two or three hundred yards" and then walked away. All around the valley was new construction, including conical towers that resembled oil derricks surrounded by hay bales. The man stated that he wondered if they were related to the practice of kendō. Overall, the man reported that the area had changed significantly.

Walking back into the city, the man reportedly carried his lunch, a large foil tray of mac-and-cheese. As he walked through the crowd at a bus stop, the man states that he stopped eating, as he remembered how uncomfortable it was to eat in public. The macaroni was described as "hot" and the man reported that he ate it with a white plastic fork.

Packing awaited

LOS ANGELES — A local man reported today that several other people were waiting for him to pack up. He stated that the others had already packed, and were waiting out of view near the door to his downtown loft. The man was allegedly looking at pins and needles that were stored in a bedspread, and "trying to get organized."

. . . . . .

Mall toured

In charge of "hyper" child

FRANCE — A U.S. man reported today that he walked around a large retail and residential complex in France today, accompanied by his brother and "some new French friends." The man described looking at the facade of the building, and stated that he was in charge of a "hyper" child for some time.

. . . . . .

Uneven student mentorship

Seafood 21 theme song performed

OTTAWA, CANADA — A visitor to the capital city reported today that he was "hanging out" with a new university student. The student was described as "chubby," with longish hair, and wearing a sweatshirt. The man stated that he wanted to give the student good advice, "but I couldn't think of anything." Later, the student sang the Seafood 21 theme song, which the witness stated "sounded more like a blues song."

The man reported that he was in a car with the student, the student's father, and an older female friend or relative, headed east of downtown. The man allegedly told the group, "When I was here before, none of these trains existed." The group witnessed an airplane land on a suburban street, just a few blocks from them, on the left side of the car. The man stated that he told the group, "Isn't it wonderful just to be starting out, to be able to do anything." The student's father reportedly laughed in response.

A serious event

CITY — A man reported tonight that in preparation to attend an event that he described as "fairly serious," he spent a lot of time choosing an outfit. At the event, a high school friend informed him that he wasn't spending enough time with the women who wanted to talk to him, so he attempted to do so.

Toilet drama at academic's house

Alarm gives confusing instructions

TOKAI REGION, JAPAN — A man reported staying at the home of a Japanese academic, but that the host hadn't cleaned up, leaving "a mess." When using the home's toilet, the man stated that it "jammed," and an alarm sounded, and a recording told him to "attach the hose and put the end out the window." The man reports that he didn't know

where the hose was, and that the toilet valve sprayed into the bathtub in order to fix the toilet clog. The man then had to drain the tub, and reportedly spoke with his host in French. There was also allegedly a third person present, but "the guy seemed left out."

Alien research project breakthrough

Full ride in academia

LOCAL — Returning to academic life after many years away, a local man reported that he was back on campus temporarily to study. He stated that he "loved the experience" and made friends. The man allegedly got involved with an alien research project breakthrough. The man stated that he planned to return to paid work after a week, but that a colleague offered him "a full ride" as a researcher after the man told him how much he was enjoying academia.

Index

Numbers

1930s **77**
1940s **47, 164**
1950s **86, 94, 107**
1960s **37, 44, 70, 76, 149, 214**
1970s **11, 15, 48, 55, 111, 120, 149, 175, 230**
1980s **141, 193**
2000s **60**

A

academia **87, 123, 126, 194, 218, 227, 233, 234, 235**
accelerator (automobile) **32, 53**
Accra, Ghana **67**
acid **21, 82**
advertising **44, 83, 208**

air-conditioning **19, 35**
aircraft **12, 15, 57, 82, 88, 130, 142, 231, 234**
  707 **183**
  737 **87**
  Cessna **178**
  Concorde **58**
airports **72, 87, 119, 130, 140, 145**
  Calgary, Canada **47**
  LAX **48, 65, 72, 81, 89, 165, 213**
  Paris Charles de Gaulle **131**
  San Francisco **230**
  Tokyo Narita **141, 217**
alarms **90, 106, 122, 148, 234**
albinos **52**

alcohol
  beer **54, 59, 185**
  cocktails **83**
    manhattan **198**
    margarita **124**
  wine **152**
alcoholism **94, 152, 198**
alfredo sauce **34**
aliens **12, 72, 82, 91, 102, 104, 122, 171, 206, 235**
alligator boots.
  See boots
all-terrain vehicles **20**
aluminum.
  See metals
amputations **75**
amusement parks **23, 46, 214**
anger **27, 29, 32, 110, 116, 119, 141, 146, 161, 202**
anime **193**

answering machines **35**
antiques **16**
ants **36**
apocalypses **102.**
See also doomsday
archaeologists **128**
architecture **12,
19, 44, 66, 75, 86,
87, 130, 163, 178,
221, 233**
arenas. *See* stadiums and arenas
Arizona **49**
art
abstract **228**
album **88**
modern **228**
artificial intelligence **2**
artworks **228**
paintings **14, 29,
38**
sculptures **178**
aspirins **184**
Athens, Greece **31**
athletic wear **17**
Atlanta **143**
Atlantic Ocean **227**
ATMs **55, 157, 232**
atomic energy.
See nuclear power
atomic waste.
See nuclear waste
atomic weapons.
See nuclear weapons
attics **66**

auditoriums **83,
225**
Austen, Jane **158**
Australia **16, 114,
142, 185, 189, 190,
214, 225**
Aztec (people,
culture) **197**

B

Baby Strax (band)
9
baggage **27, 30, 66,
126, 142, 149, 217**
baking **112, 132**
balconies **74, 147,
164**
Bangalore **51**
banknotes **54,
170, 186, 232.** *See
also* cash
banks **21, 133, 157,
203, 224, 232**
barbecue **114**
bars (entertainment venue) **25,
80, 83, 100, 124,
125, 186**
bartenders **94**
Bastille **92**
bathrooms (home)
**19, 34, 84, 129,
137, 182, 202,
205.** *See also* restrooms (public)
bathtubs **20**
Bay Bridge **160**
beards **176**
bedrooms **55, 56,
66, 119, 139, 145,
197, 201**
beer. *See* alcohol

bees **46, 185, 226**
Beetle (car).
See cars
bellhops **99**
Benedict XVI
(pope) **142**
Bering Strait **95**
Berkeley, Calif. **62**
Beverly Hillbillies
(TV series) **70,
183**
bicycles **21, 28, 39,
61, 97, 111, 157,
159, 180, 196, 218,
226**
Big Bear Lake,
Calif. **35**
bills (cash).
See banknotes
bilocation **117**
binders (stationery) **36**
birds **36, 113, 115**
crows **36**
giant **165, 166**
hummingbirds
206, 226
partridges **105**
puppet **166**
ravens **36**
birthdays **158.**
See also parties,
birthday
bison **17**
blackmail **159**
Black (people,
culture) **89**
blonds **24, 26, 31,
54, 66, 68, 76, 97,
124, 154, 173, 176,
196, 202, 214, 221,
226**

blood **64, 112, 123, 159**
blouses. *See* shirts and blouses
blow-dryers **152**
blow jobs **77**
blues music. *See* music
BMW. *See* cars
board games **67, 228**
boats **36, 57, 119.** *See also* ships
inflatable (Zodiac) **177**
Treasure Island, the **36**
bodies, dead. *See* corpses
bombs **123, 151**
booby-traps **14**
books **39, 86, 95, 96, 131, 135, 141, 142, 145, 154, 159, 170, 176, 193, 215**
boots **46, 62, 154**
alligator **215**
bowling **109, 217**
boxes, cardboard **130, 177, 202, 218**
brain damage **225**
brain enhancers **189**
brakes (automotive) **32, 209**
breakers (electrical) **15**
breakfast **18, 37, 40, 138**
break-ins **123, 148.** *See also* theft
bribery **23**

briefcases **130, 183**
Britain **119, 193, 210**
British (people, culture) **8, 88, 131, 148, 156, 205, 210**
broken glass. *See* glass, broken
brooms **180**
brunettes **25, 47, 54, 112, 123, 177, 196**
brush fires **48, 154**
Buckley, William F., Jr. (pundit) **10**
Budapest **63**
Buddha **78**
buildings, tall **19, 44, 75, 111, 130, 145, 148, 171, 200, 221**
bullets. *See* firearms
burglary. *See* theft
burners (cooking) **70**
buses **14, 23, 46, 54, 72, 74, 95, 145, 160, 188, 199, 211, 233**
school buses **142, 145**
butter **206**
butterflies **157**
buttocks **23, 69, 95, 180, 193**

C

cabinets **57, 155.** *See also* cupboards
cable cars **43, 126**
cable television **30**
cafés **9, 54, 97, 116, 126, 144, 182, 184, 219**
cafeterias **86, 114, 123, 214**
caffeine **89**
Calgary, Canada **47**
camelias **206**
cameras
attached to head **211, 213**
cinematic **94, 160**
still photo **50, 130**
television **187**
video **165**
camping **112, 177, 189, 212**
campus. *See* academia
canals **21, 161, 185**
candles **22, 154**
candy **24**
Canter's Deli (Los Angeles) **141**
canyons **28, 29**
captains
Captain Kirk (fictional character) **49**
navy **22**
carafes **226**
carpet **133, 179**

cars **26, 31, 34, 43, 51, 63, 67, 80, 85, 101, 109, 112, 116, 118, 121, 122, 128, 131, 147, 150, 151, 157, 159, 178, 186, 192, 194, 197, 199, 211, 213, 215, 218, 234.** *See also* trucks

BMW convertible **219**

Chevy Malibu **53**

Daihatsu Mira **31**

dune buggies **222**

Geo Metro **154**

Honda Civic **217**

Jeep Cherokee **158**

Land Rover **209**

Model T Ford **202**

muscle cars **53**

pickups. *See* trucks, pickups

Plymouth **175, 230**

police cars **106, 206**

station wagons **81**

Studebaker **41**

vans. *See* trucks, vans

Volkswagen Beetle **107, 221**

Yukon **222**

car chases **51**

cartoons **47, 157, 165, 210.** *See also* anime

cash **170, 172, 183, 232.** *See also* banknotes; *See also* coins

cashiers **51, 81, 86**

cash registers **51**

casinos **121**

castles **92, 150, 210, 211**

Catalina Island, Calif. **36**

cats **172, 229**

cat litter **179**

caverns. *See* caves

caves **71, 105**

CDs **9, 23, 88**

cell phones. *See* telephones

ceramics **70, 226**

Cessnas. *See* aircraft

chairlifts **113**

chairs

  dining **58**

  kindergarten **143**

  lawn **75, 162**

characters, Japanese **10**

Château Laurier Hotel (Ottawa, Canada) **74**

checkout. *See* cash registers

cheese **63.** *See also* mac-and-cheese

chefs **37, 170**

cherrywood **57**

Chevy. *See* cars

chicken **133**

chicken dance **192**

China **152**

Chinese (people, culture) **64, 152.** *See also* languages, non-English, Mandarin

chocolate **151**

Christmas **204, 222**

chrome. *See* metals

churches **116, 130, 143, 193**

church spires **130**

Churchill, Winston (politician) **210**

cigarettes **46**

cigarette machines **55**

cilantro **194**

cinemas **41, 87, 93, 95, 99, 148, 156.** *See also* theaters

citations (legal document) **117**

city hall **52**

civil disobedience. *See* protests

Cleveland, Ohio **128**

Clifford (fictional character) **39**

cliffs **126, 178**

cloaks **60**

clover **108**

CNN **31**

coasters **133**

coats 8, 47, 180,
219
raincoats 149
trench coats 43,
204, 232
cocktails. *See* alcohol
coffee 9, 37, 54, 74,
128, 230
coins 8, 29
cola 98
Cold War 48, 157
colors
black 9, 28, 29,
36, 44, 47, 48,
55, 75, 78, 87,
91, 108, 146,
163, 190, 193,
202, 209
black and white
67, 89, 108, 204
blues 8, 11, 41,
52, 63, 65, 70,
74, 77, 86, 102,
106, 126, 131,
151, 154, 157,
177
#00A294 78
#3EB7E3 25
aqua blue 42
blue-green 184
dark blue 151
electric blue
53
indigo 63
pastel blue 78
powder blue
15
royal blue 63
sky blue 25
tile blue 42

browns 25, 38,
46, 195
tan 221
grays 9, 16, 20,
25, 29, 77, 89,
92, 94, 102, 172,
209
crunchy gray
90
greens 9, 11, 14,
18, 19, 20, 53,
87, 88, 133, 160,
167, 188, 205
blue-green 184
lime green 222
pastel green 78
oranges 77, 131
Day-Glo orange 12
pinks 41, 52, 56,
61, 132, 192
fuchsia 189
purples 14, 17,
38, 171, 189,
222
reds 9, 28, 29, 31,
38, 39, 44, 48,
60, 74, 104, 126,
151, 152, 158,
171, 178, 193,
199, 209, 215,
220, 230. *See
also* redheads
bright red 70
dark red 46,
90, 196
fire-engine red
215
Selenicas 76
whites 9, 38, 42,
44, 195, 214,
215, 222, 233

cream 38
off-white 52
yellows 19, 46,
50, 102, 157
bright yellow
183
#C2B515 78
Cedar Blond
76
dusty yellow
190
gold 40
hot yellow 217
lemon yellow
90
mustard yellow
209
pastel yellow
78
peach 56
comedians 59, 131,
160
comedy 18, 99
coming out 196
commandos 219
communism 156
community service
110
computers 67, 84,
89, 107
laptops 135, 149
concerts 83, 95
Concorde. *See* aircraft
concrete 19, 46, 58,
105, 190
condominiums
118
conspiracies 2,
143, 148
convenience stores
93

cookies **132, 195, 210**

cooking **17, 19, 169, 171, 194**

coolness (fashionable) **9, 46, 58, 74, 76, 171, 177**

coolness (tolerant demeanor) **129, 217**

corpses **46, 218**

correction fluid **138, 158**

cosmetic surgery **34, 61**

cosmological symmetry **60**

cosmology **60**

Cotswolds, UK **193**

country music. *See* music

coupons **18**

courtrooms **147**

crackers **59**

crashes
aircraft **178, 188, 209**
auto **11, 38, 65, 70, 99, 108, 144, 200, 209, 215, 219, 225**

crazy. *See* mental illness

crepes **151**

Croatia **187**

crocodiles **60**

crowds **15, 19, 54, 59, 62, 106, 110, 148, 156, 174, 210, 233**

crows **36**

crucifixes **170**

Cunning Dolls, the (band) **88**

cupboards **168, 196.** *See also* cabinets

cups. *See* dishes

cycling. *See* bicycles

D

Daihatsu. *See* cars

Dalmatians. *See* dogs

dams **164, 187**

dance **70**
chicken dance **192**
pole dance **62**
the rage **79**

dark hair. *See* brunettes

death **28, 77, 108, 113, 159, 176, 185.** *See also* corpses; *See also* murder

debit cards **55**

deer **76, 112**

Denmark **180**

Denny's (restaurant) **37**

department stores **37, 44**

deposit, bank **204, 224, 232**

depression. *See* mental illness

deserts **46, 49, 95, 129, 139, 151**

desserts **151**

detectives **65, 66, 143, 206, 229**

devil **18, 109, 180**

diapers **83**

diaries. *See* journals

dinners. *See* parties, dinner

Dion, Céline (singer) **199**

dioramas **169, 171**

disability **42, 54**

diseases **27, 146**

dishes **30, 43, 217**
cups **37, 142, 177**
mugs **63, 168**
plates **70, 194**

diving (pool) **49, 197**

diving (scuba) **36, 186**

DJs **79**

dō (道) **126, 233**

doctors **75, 88**

dogfights (aviation) **142**

dogs **11, 17, 32, 43, 113, 125, 157**
cartoon **39**
Dalmatians **108**
German shepherds **137, 146**
greyhounds **180**
terriers **128, 146**

dolls **88, 132**

doomsday **210, 231**

doppelgängers **31, 52, 61, 105.** *See also* twins

dragons **179**

drainpipes **194**

drug dealers **105, 169**

drugs (illicit) **168.** *See also* medications

marijuana **105**

drunkeness **102, 115, 152, 198**

Dublin, Ireland **140**

ducks **57, 188**

dumps (landfill) **89, 129**

dune buggies **222**

dyes **59, 102, 130**

E

earphones **61.** *See also* headphones

Earth (planet) **49, 57, 69, 102, 122**

earth (soil) **46, 85**

earthquakes **20, 32, 85, 104, 187**

Ebsen, Buddy (actor) **70**

eggs **102, 179**

Eiffel Tower **12**

elderly people **17, 30, 36, 68, 78, 95, 96, 129, 156, 193, 205, 211, 212**

elevators **37, 110, 134, 145**

elves **85**

email **68, 224**

embalming **79**

embers **155**

emergencies **123, 162, 165, 200, 226**

Empire State Building (New York City) **148**

English as a second language (education) **107, 213**

English language **69, 87, 125, 131, 219**

envelopes **53, 79**

escalators **23, 101, 146, 163**

Euro (fashion) **105**

Europe **58, 75, 87, 211**

European (people) **95, 122**

European Union **88**

eviction **119, 154**

examinations. *See* tests

explosions **14, 19, 48, 57, 59, 72, 166.** *See also* mushroom clouds

eyeglasses **10, 22, 25, 34, 61, 96, 173, 189.** *See also* sunglasses

F

fabrics **59, 126, 179, 190, 229**

Fairfax Avenue, Los Angeles **54, 141, 224**

fangs **67**

farmers markets **231**

fashion **12, 42, 67, 108, 120, 126, 189**

Fashion District (Los Angeles) **42**

fat. *See* obesity

faxes **109**

fences **38, 78, 208, 211**

ferns **35**

Filipino (people, culture) **221**

film directors **97, 165**

film industry **39, 119, 145, 158, 160, 165, 169, 184**

filming **184, 187**

film noir **204**

film (photography) **50**

film screenings **83, 95, 97**

fire **32, 48, 71, 92, 144, 154, 155, 172, 195**

firearms. *See also* gunfights

ammunition **64**

bullets **28, 48, 106**

gunfire **166**

handguns **64, 106, 134**

machine guns **77**

magazines **64**

rifles **152, 180**

shells **180**

shotguns **37, 180**

fire extinguishers **228**

fireplaces **167**

fish **12, 42, 165**

fistfights **116**

flames. *See* fire

flannel 77
flaxseed 179
fleas 182
flight attendants
41, 58, 81
flights 15, 47, 48,
58, 87, 88, 92, 119,
138, 140, 142, 160,
184, 195, 209
Flintstones (TV
series) 214
flooding 21, 125,
188, 220
Florida 20, 203
folk music.
See music, folk
folk singers 89,
107, 177
food carts 232
Ford. *See* cars
fountains 12, 49,
124, 135
fractals 130
France 93, 97, 125,
161, 219, 233
freeways 67, 160,
219
French (people,
culture) 32, 97,
120, 130, 157,
170, 208, 233. *See
also* languages,
non-English
Freud, Sigmund
(psychologist) 1
frogs 19
Fukuroi, Japan
135
full moon 114

G

gangsters 80, 93.
See also orga-
nized crime
garages 26, 43, 52,
128, 180, 211
garbage 20, 70,
129, 155
garbage bags 133
garbage cans 196
garbage trucks
129, 155
gardens 37, 44, 66,
140, 157, 168, 206,
222, 227
Garment Center
(New York City)
139
gas leaks 75
gas masks 121, 123
gas stations 121,
187
gender issues 51,
164, 167, 205, 210,
219
genkan (玄関) 86
Geo. *See* cars
German (people,
culture) 12, 75,
92, 125, 146, 175.
See also languag-
es, non-English
German shep-
herds. *See* dogs
Germany 121
Getty Center (Los
Angeles) 201
ghosts 135
Gilligan's Island
(TV series) 37

glass, broken 76,
173, 200
glasses (dishes)
48, 152
glasses (eyewear).
See eyeglasses
Global Positioning
System 139
globes 100
gods 3, 18, 63
Golden Gate
Bridge (San
Francisco) 39
gold foil 79
gold mining 185
golf 102
golf courses 102
gorillas 137
grammar 122
granite 12, 55
grapes 157
gravel 11, 28, 220
gravestones 128
graveyards 128
GRE. *See* tests,
academic
Greece 31, 93, 186
Greek (language,
people) 88, 93
green tea. *See* tea
greyhounds (dogs).
See dogs
grocery stores.
See supermar-
kets; *See* markets
guns. *See* firearms
gynecologists 199

H

Haida (culture)
178
haircuts 15

hairstyles 47
  1970s 15
  mod 177
  perms 173
  pompadours 173
Halifax, Canada 9
Halloween 124
hallucinations 94
hamsters 10
handbags 44, 191
handguns. *See* firearms
handstands 187
hangars 59
hardwood 40, 179
harps 16
Hasidim 186
hats 120, 142, 180, 188, 192, 210
headlights 128
headphones 166. *See also* earphones
Hebrew. *See* languages, non-English
hedges 31
helicopters 115
helmets 61
high-rises. *See* buildings, tall
highways 33, 40, 131, 155, 161, 178, 195, 196. *See also* freeways
hijacking 188
hippies 33, 38, 66, 72
hitchhiking 33
Hitler 121, 210
HOA fees 118

Hollywood Boulevard, Los Angeles 199, 229
Hollywood (Los Angeles) 90, 117, 142, 199, 221
homework 101, 131
homophobia 32, 35, 91, 100
Honda. *See* cars
honeymoons 176
Hong Kong 229
hookups 24, 25, 56, 83, 92, 116, 144, 161, 176, 202, 214
horses 23, 152, 175
hospitals 32, 68, 72, 197, 200, 226
  emergency rooms 226
hotels 24, 42, 63, 74, 82, 85, 93, 99, 138, 141, 143, 150, 163, 164, 176, 178, 204, 208, 213, 216, 219, 231
hot springs 59, 62, 93, 156
hummingbirds 206, 226
humor 69, 86, 159, 165, 166, 170, 171, 199
hyacinths 206
hyperactivity 233

I

ibuprofen 201
ice cream 168

ID (documents) 43, 111, 141. *See also* passports
incense 15
India 50
Indonesia 75
insects 19, 151, 157, 167, 182
insincerity 81, 204
interdimensional entities 135
interpretation (languages). *See* translation
Ireland 140
Irish (people, culture) 135, 228
iron. *See* metals
ironing boards 16
Israel 95, 151
Israeli (people, culture) 97

J

jackets. *See* coats
Japan 8, 43, 59, 67, 134, 135, 158, 175, 185, 209, 215
Japanese (people, culture) 16, 36, 44, 55, 81, 86, 97, 136, 159, 164, 169, 170, 173, 193, 220, 231, 234. *See also* languages, non-English
Japanese yen 29, 98, 170
javelins 118
jeans. *See* pants
Jeep. *See* cars

jewelry 43. *See also* lockets
Jewish (people, culture) 74, 186
jogging 17, 170
journalists 90, 142, 149, 231
journals 145
jousting 175
Jung, Carl (psychologist) 1
junk food 99
junk mail 133
junkyards 41

K

Kakegawa, Japan 149
Kananaskis Country, Canada 152
kanji (漢字). *See* characters, Japanese
kappa 136
kendō 233
Kevlar 162
keys 84, 122, 132, 147, 170, 172
kimonos 213
kindergartens 143, 150
kissing 25, 32, 56, 124, 205, 214
kitsch 22
Kmart (retail store) 44
knives 26, 46, 72, 171, 201
Korean (language). *See* languages, non-English
kotatsu (炬燵) 134

L

labels (stationery) 53, 115, 186
lamb (meat) 114
lambs (animal) 122
Land Rover. *See* cars
landslides 29
languages, non-English 31, 122, 125, 148
French 16, 125, 235
German 121
Hebrew 97
Japanese 10, 23, 44, 98, 125, 165, 208. *See also* characters, Japanese
Korean 36
Lamb 122
Latin 69
Mandarin 64
laptop computers. *See* computers
Larchmont (Los Angeles) 52
larvae 190
Las Vegas, Nev. 121
Latin (language). *See* languages, non-English
Latter-day Saints 106, 176
lattice 133
laundry 15, 23, 147
lawn chairs. *See* chairs

LAX airport. *See* airports
laxatives 72
legal jargon 69
letters (documents) 64, 114, 119, 133, 145, 149. *See also* mail
letters (Latin alphabet) 9, 11, 230
libraries 71
Library Tower (Los Angeles) 111
Liffey River, Ireland 140
liner notes 9
lockets 41
London 132, 215
luggage. *See* baggage
lumber 180

M

mac-and-cheese 233
machine guns. *See* firearms
mafia 63, 183. *See also* organized crime
magazines (ammunition). *See* firearms
magazines (print) 12, 69, 136, 149, 166, 214
magnets 163
mahogany 57
maids 99

mail 64, 104, 133, 194, 205. *See also* letters
Maine 229
makeovers 61
makeup 19, 74
mall (shopping) 69, 74, 98, 156, 183, 208, 220, 228, 233
Mandarin (language). *See* languages, non-English
Manhattan (borough). *See* New York City
manhattan (cocktail) 198
Manitoba 26, 96
manners, bad 27, 94, 110, 141, 145, 184, 203, 216
maps 33, 51, 69, 135, 151, 186, 226, 228
marathons 133
marches 43. *See also* protests
margaritas 124
marijuana. *See* drugs (illicit)
markets 38, 59, 68, 147. *See also* supermarkets
Mars (planet) 48, 162
mathematics 116, 178, 222
mayonnaise 179
maypoles 62

medians (highway) 220
medications 24, 70, 82, 94, 174, 191
  aspirin 184
  esquerida 94
  esqureida 94
  ibuprofen 201
  Vicodin 174
meetings 104, 125, 132, 138
  diplomatic 161
  international 19
  public 225
  school 214
  secret 82
  think-tank 190
  twelve-step 167, 224
Melbourne 189
mental illness 26, 40, 72, 200
  depression 26, 40
mental states 126, 149, 179
mentorship 32, 233
metals 102, 168, 219, 232
  aluminum 78
  chrome 53
  gold 79, 185
  iron 232
  steel 20
  tin 42
metal detectors 81
Mexico 46, 149
Miami 20
mice (animal) 226
migraines 174

military 12, 115, 142. *See also* navy; *See also* paramilitary; *See also* commandos; *See also* Pentagon; *See also* soldiers
Miracle Mile (Los Angeles) 54, 191
mirrors 29, 41, 48, 52, 137, 184
missiles 195
Mississippi River 96
Miss Piggy (fictional character) 69
moisturizer 54
Mojave Desert 139
Montana 106
Mont Blanc 93
Montreal 10, 46
moon 102, 113
mopeds. *See* motorcycles
motorcycles 92, 118
mountains 3, 105, 117, 173, 190, 209, 211
  Mont Blanc 93
  Mount Fuji 8, 163
  Mount Rushmore 94
  Rockies 16
  San Bernardinos 35
  San Gabriels 54
  Sierras 62

Yatsugatakes (Nagano) **23**
Mount Fuji **8, 163**
Mount Rushmore **94**
mouse (computer) **84**
movies **16, 41, 79, 94, 99, 109, 114, 119, 156, 160, 210.** *See also* film
movie theaters. *See* cinemas
mud **29, 68, 141, 155, 194**
mugs. *See* dishes
murder **79, 105, 147, 159, 185**
muscle cars. *See* cars
mushroom clouds **48, 231**
music
   blues **219, 234**
   British **88**
   country **199**
   folk **16, 89, 107, 177**
   funky **70**
   pop **80, 149**
music videos **165**
muslin **56**
mustaches **25, 48, 164**
mute **152**
muumuus **214**

N

Nagano Prefecture, Japan **23**
nails (hands) **150**

nails (hardware) **133**
Narita Airport. *See* airports
Native Americans **24**
navy **12, 22**
Nazis **121, 156, 210**
Neanderthals **76**
neckties **197**
needles (sewing) **233**
needles (turntable) **79**
New Age **3**
newspapers **50, 68, 147, 194, 230**
New York City **18, 44, 69, 71, 72, 139, 146, 148, 227**
New York, upstate **39, 113**
New Zealand **89**
nightclubs **9, 12, 130, 174**
noodles **34, 179**
North Carolina **190**
notes **43, 93**
   left under windshield wiper **117, 121, 213**
   mental **231**
Nova Scotia **9, 33**
nuclear power **12, 82**
nuclear waste **89**
nuclear weapons **12, 72**
nuts **10, 11**

O

obesity **18, 34, 52, 76, 78, 90, 99, 174, 177, 187, 189, 203, 228, 233**
office towers. *See* buildings, tall
oil derricks **232**
Oi River, Japan **135**
Old West **185**
olive oil **194**
Omaha, Neb. **72**
onions **17, 128**
opium **30**
orange juice **80, 98**
Orange Julius (retailer) **98**
organized crime **8, 63, 80, 183**
orgies **56, 123**
Osaka, Japan **8**
Otki Prison **148**
Ottawa, Canada **15, 21, 74, 92, 95, 108, 112, 129, 184, 194, 210, 233**

P

Pacific Ocean **12, 22, 148, 185**
paddleboards **55**
paint **29, 88, 92, 228**
paintbrushes **104**
pallets **58**
Palm Springs, Calif. **41, 129**
pancakes **19, 38**
pantographs **120**

pants 44, 77, 109, 208
  chinos 195
  jeans 18, 23, 147, 180, 193, 195
paper clips 85–86
Papua New Guinea 143
paramilitary 24
Paris 92, 125, 129, 130
parking 16, 41, 43, 67, 85, 109, 112, 116, 128, 154, 155, 157, 178, 192, 197, 213, 230
parking lots and structures 121, 130, 133, 134, 146, 171, 205, 221
parks
  city 21, 43, 67, 76, 95, 126, 172, 232
  national 31
  regional 96
Parliament (Ottawa, Canada) 74, 194, 210
parties
  birthday 94, 116
  dinner 36, 119, 159, 169, 172, 216
  dress 69
  house 104, 113, 124, 126, 196, 200, 204
  street 81, 135
partridges 68, 105
Pasadena, Calif. 230

passports 141, 230
pasta. See noodles
pay phones.
  See telephone booths
PBS 231
peanuts 11
Pentagon 161
perms. See hairstyles
Philadelphia 63, 67
phone books.
  See telephone books
phone booths.
  See telephones, pay
photography 50, 158
photos 11, 36, 38, 49–50, 70, 141, 142, 158, 166, 213
pi (π) 222
pie 54, 112
pine (wood) 58
pirates 12–13
pizza 221
plaid 44, 188
plastic 11, 22, 81, 229, 233
plates. See dishes
playground equipment 179
  slides 55, 124
Plymouth. See cars
pole dancing 62
police 15, 17, 23, 30, 43, 65, 131, 141, 143, 145, 149, 155, 160, 169, 200, 211, 225, 229, 230

police cars.
  See cars
police stations 71
Polish (people) 68
politics 57, 77, 89, 210
polo shirts.
  See shirts and blouses
pompadours.
  See hairstyles
ponds 37, 165
pools. See swimming pools
pool (table game) 25
popes 142
porcelain 39
pornography 193, 201
postal system 53
postcards 38
potatoes 99, 167
potholes 178
potters 180
pottery 142
power outages 93, 230
power steering 218
Pregnant, Peggy (musician) 89
Pregnant, Priggy (musician) 89
Presley, Elvis (musician) 80
prisons 86, 91, 148
professors. See academia
projector, film 114
protests 19, 28, 203
Providence, R.I. 128

psych evaluations **226**

psychic power **35, 100**

psychics **3, 39–40, 216**

psychologists **56, 209**

psychology **1, 91**

psychotherapy **121**

public baths **96.** *See also* hot springs

public protests **43.** *See also* civil disobedience

pumpkins **80**

punches **116.** *See also* fistfights

punks **132**

puppets **166, 178**

purses. *See* handbags

Q

Quebec **21, 169, 208**

R

racism **77, 89**

raincoats. *See* coats

ranches **231**

ranges (cooking) **71, 128, 151, 179, 196**

rats **52**

ravens **36**

razors **123**

Reagan, Ronald (politician) **141**

reality TV **174, 187**

recessions **141**

redheads **18, 25, 29, 65, 162, 222**

rednecks **17, 189**

refrigerators **58, 163**

reincarnation **204, 225**

renovations **19, 66, 74, 155, 165, 218**

research **22, 114, 235.** *See also* scientists

restrooms (public) **30, 34, 39, 46, 89, 138, 167, 171, 174, 183, 193, 208, 227.** *See also* bathrooms (home)

reunions
family **120, 162**
personal **98, 175**
school **192**
workplace **91, 205, 212**

Rhode Island **128**

rice crackers **59**

Rideau Canal (Ottawa, Canada) **21, 185**

rifles. *See* firearms

rivers **111**
Mississippi **96**
Oi **135**
Warashina **187**

robbery. *See* theft

Roberts, Jane **3–5**

robots **74, 219**

rodents **52**

Roman, ancient (people, culture) **104**

Rosa Chá (designer) **149**

rubber **119**

rubber gloves **183**

rudeness. *See* manners, bad

Russia **161**

Russian (people) **157, 183, 187**

RVs **24, 33–34**

S

sadness **40, 74, 78**

saints, Catholic **152**

Saints, Latter-day. *See* Latter-day Saints

Saint George **152**

Saint Sebastian **152**

salt-and-pepper hair **66**

San Diego **97**

San Francisco **39, 42, 78, 116, 126, 137, 160, 182, 191, 230**

sandwiches **102**

Santa Catalina, Calif. *See* Catalina Island, Calif.

Santa Monica Boulevard, Los Angeles **159, 224**

Santorini, Greece **93**

saris **213**

Saskatchewan **150**

scarves **168, 210**

school buses. *See* buses

scientists **61, 82, 128.** *See also* research

Scooby-Doo (fictional character) **42**

Scotland **211**

Scottish (people, culture) **99**

screwdriver (tool) **28, 56**

scuba diving. *See* diving

Seafood 21 **234**

search parties **82, 133**

seeds **11**

flaxseed **179**

Seibu (department store) **37**

sembé (crackers) **59**

senior citizens. *See* elderly people

servers (food service) **54, 110, 143, 184, 230**

Seth Material **3–5**

sex **76, 89, 121.** *See also* hookups

sexual overtures **196, 212**

Shaggy (fictional character) **42**

sharks **42**

Sharpies (stationery) **158**

sheep **102**

shells (ammunition) **180**

shift (garment) **215**

shinkansen. *See* trains

ships **75, 121, 148, 188.** *See also* boats

navy **12, 22**

nuclear **12**

Titanic **227**

shirts and blouses **63, 126, 147, 174, 189, 193, 205**

polo **65**

sweatshirts **233**

tank tops **77**

T-shirts **42, 206**

undershirts **77**

shit **100, 113, 171, 195, 202**

Shizuoka City, Japan **164**

Shizuoka Prefecture, Japan **135**

shoes **47, 86, 90, 95, 120, 172, 208, 211**

shootings **63, 77, 152, 165, 180.** *See also* firearms

shoplifting. *See* theft

shopping carts **51**

shotguns. *See* firearms

showers **9, 20, 30, 189, 195, 202**

Siberia **95**

Sierra Springs, Calif. **62**

signs **37, 177**

car badges **42**

door **14**

hotel **204**

neon **204**

parking **116, 192**

retail **199**

street **142**

warning **230**

Singapore **147**

singing **120**

sit-ins **203.** *See also* protests

skiing

cross-country **152**

downhill **18, 93, 129**

resorts **9, 174**

sledgehammers **17**

slides. *See* playground equipment; *See also* waterslides

sluices **55**

Smith, Anna Nicole (TV personality) **147**

smoke (air pollution) **15, 48, 188, 231**

smoking (inhalation) **30, 44, 190**

snacks **59, 101**

snakes **67, 96**

snow **9, 10, 83, 112, 119, 178, 218**

sobriety **94, 185, 198, 220**

sockets, electrical **152**

sockets, eye **28**

socks **208**
software **84, 166**
soldiers **63.**
  See military
Somali (people,
  culture) **162**
songs **11, 19, 107,**
  120, 121, 199, 214,
  219, 234
sound waves **157**
South African
  (people) **27**
South Dakota **94,**
  231
Southeast Asia **38,**
  143, 197
South Pasadena,
  Calif. **70**
south pole **71**
space **48, 195**
spaceflight **58, 162,**
  195
spaceships **48**
space shuttle **188,**
  195
space-time **60–61**
sparks **77, 80, 155**
spas **21.** *See*
  also hot springs
spit **112, 201**
squid **42, 99**
squid ink **99**
squirrels **105**
  ground squirrels
  147
stadiums and
  arenas **39–40, 69,**
  121, 133
staircases **14, 18,**
  25, 55, 66, 84, 86,
  135, 143, 174, 190,
  206, 219

Star Trek (TV se-
  ries) **48**
static **79**
station wagons.
  See cars
steel. *See* metals
stoats **52**
stoops **76**
stoves. *See* ranges
  (cooking)
strippers **62, 76**
Studebaker.
  See cars
subsidence (archi-
  tecture) **178**
suburbia **23, 59,**
  78, 234
subway trains.
  See trains
sugar **226**
suitcases. *See* bag-
  gage
suits **20, 85, 188,**
  204, 222
summer camp
  106, 120, 146
sun **111, 216**
sunglasses **61, 91,**
  96
supermarkets **51,**
  80, 101, 137, 141,
  194, 212. *See*
  also markets;
  See also farmers
  markets
  Trader Joe's **141,**
  230
surfboards **148**
suspenders **77**
sweaters **11, 138,**
  193

sweatshirts.
  See shirts and
  blouses
swimming pools
  49, 63, 93, 113,
  120, 176, 197, 202,
  217, 218, 220
swimwear **42, 50,**
  197

T

Tahiti **60**
tails **109**
Taiwanese (people,
  culture) **115**
tampons **87**
tanker trucks.
  See trucks
tank tops.
  See shirts and
  blouses
tarot cards **168**
tattoos **124, 139**
taxes **22**
tax forms **158, 220**
tea **31, 230**
  green tea **193**
teachers **16, 25, 34,**
  131, 148, 213, 231
teeth **42, 62, 136**
telekinesis **66, 215**
telephone books
  85–86
telephone booths.
  See telephones,
  pay
telephones
  calls **58, 85, 93,**
  108, 117, 137,
  208, 224, 231

cellular **47, 64, 89, 111, 132, 144, 157**
desk **68, 144, 160, 229**
numbers **104, 182, 203**
pay **17, 29, 32, 35**
wiring **117**
tents **95**
terriers. *See* dogs
terrorists **87, 134, 164**
testes **108**
tests, academic **99, 114**
 Graduate Record Examinations (GRE) **107**
tests, medical **68**
Thatcher, Margaret (politician) **193**
theaters **216**. *See also* cinemas
theft **72, 90, 99, 110, 117**
 burglary **43, 92, 183**
 robbery **100, 149, 175**
 shoplifting **43**
theme parks. *See* amusement parks
theme songs **214, 233**
thieves **43, 150, 183**
think tanks **190**
third eye **48**

Tic Tacs (candy) **112**
tie-dyeing **59**
ties. *See* neckties
tigers **68, 165, 203**
time travel **12, 76, 82, 107, 193, 204, 214**
tin. *See* metals
Tin Tin (fictional character) **210**
Titanic (ship) **227**
toads **140**
toast (drink to in recognition) **158, 166**
tofu **169**
toilet paper **215**
toilets **19, 21, 34, 44, 100, 150, 183, 215, 234**. *See also* restrooms (public); *See also* bathrooms (home)
Tōkaidō Main Line **99, 185**
Tokyo **55, 59, 185**
toll booths **23**
tomatoes **17, 89, 140**
tongues **25, 184**
toothbrushes **195**
tornadoes **51, 131**
Toronto **59, 80**
tourism **9, 16, 39–40, 97, 146, 148, 184, 186, 189, 199, 210, 214, 233**
tournaments **120**
towers (buildings). *See* buildings, tall

tow trucks. *See* trucks
toys **57, 66**
track marks **126**
tractors **11**
Trader Joe's. *See* supermarkets
trailers **162, 188**
trains **27, 64, 75, 91, 97, 99, 111, 116, 120, 130, 134, 190, 234**
 bullet **134, 149, 209**
 subway **37, 68, 90, 139**
train stations **68, 80, 117, 134, 209, 217**
 Kakegawa, Japan **149**
 Union Station (Los Angeles) **58, 220**
translation **125, 163, 219**
trash. *See* garbage
trench coats. *See* coats
trucks **28, 145**
 flatbeds **17**
 freight **196**
 fuel **144**
 garbage **129, 155**
 pickups **118, 140, 183, 199**
 semis **33, 221**
 tankers **57**
 three-quarter-ton **70**
 tow **198**
 vans **217**

T-shirts. *See* shirts and blouses
turntables (audio equipment) **79**
turtles **105, 136**
twins **55, 61, 102, 149, 205.** *See also* doppelgängers

U

UCLA **218**
undershirts. *See* shirts and blouses
underwear **22, 78, 147, 217**
uniforms **24, 87, 110, 169**
United Kingdom. *See* Britain
urinals **174**
urine **113, 208**
UV light **38**

V

Vail, Colo. **174**
Vancouver, Canada **177**
van Gogh, Vincent (artist) **18**
vegetables **16, 167, 220**
Velcro **162**
Velveeta (processed cheese) **63**
vertigo **198**
Vicodin. *See* medications
Vietnam **197**

Volkswagen Beetle. *See* cars

W

waffles **169**
Warashina River, Japan **187**
warehouses **228**
Warsaw **129**
Washington, D.C. **69, 161, 169**
waterslides **55**
waves **140, 185, 220**
weapons. *See* firearms; *See* bombs; *See* knives
weddings **79, 176**
West Hollywood, Calif. **43, 53, 120, 213**
Westwood (Los Angeles) **218**
wheelchairs **8, 28, 32, 168**
whips **156, 175**
wild boars **58**
windows (glass)
  aircraft **59, 82**
  apartment **198**
  building **19, 89, 228**
  bus **75, 160**
  car **80**
  house **55, 211, . 222, 234**
  kitchen **178, 226**
  retail **35, 141, 199**
  train **64**
Windows (software) **166**

wine. *See* alcohol
winter **83, 134, 146, 174, 191, 218**
winter clothes **47, 148, 192, 219**
wires **117, 120**
Wite-Out. *See* correction fluid
wolves **58**
World War II **12, 121, 157**
worms **19, 190**
Wyoming **231**

X

X-rays **165**

Y

Yakuza **8, 80, 159.** *See also* organized crime
yang **196**
yankī **173**
yarmulkes **186**
yin **197**
yogurt **132**

Z

Zodiac. *See* boats
zombies **48, 53, 218**